It's Called a

BREAKUP

Because It's

BROKEN

It's Called a
BREAKUP
Because It's
BROKEN

The Smart Girl's
Breakup Buddy

Greg Behrendt &
Amiira Ruotola-Behrendt

HarperElement
An Imprint of HarperCollins*Publishers*
77–85 Fulham Palace Road,
Hammersmith, London W6 8JB

The website address is: www.thorsonselement.com

and *HarperElement* are trademarks of
HarperCollins*Publishers* Ltd

First published in the US by Broadway Books 2005
This edition published by HarperElement 2006

4

Book design by Chris Welch

A catalogue record of this book is
available from the British Library

ISBN-13   978-0-00-722518-7
ISBN-10   0-00-722518-0

Printed and bound in Great Britain by
Clays Ltd, St Ives plc

This book is for the True and Mighty.

CONTENTS

It's Called a

BREAKUP

Because It's

BROKEN

GREG'S INTRO

*L*ong, long ago in a sad galaxy far far away, I was dating this stone-cold Superfox. And when I say dating, what I really mean to say is that I was sick in love with her, while she thought I was a "really good guy." Needless to say, things fell apart. We had one of those awkward breakups where you're living together and sleeping in the same bed but you're not going out anymore. "Excuse me, I know you're seeing someone else, but can I have some of that pillow?" Ouch. Who does that? Me, as it turns out. I was so smitten (read: in love with not getting what I want) with this girl that I was sure that if I was just near her, taking any crumb thrown my way and drinking myself to sleep every night, she'd find me attractive again and want my sad ass back. Well, it wasn't long before she decided to bail. So off she went to New York to pursue her career, and, more important, her new man.

Now, you'd think that after someone leaves you for another person and moves to another city across the country you would get that it's over, because it is. But I didn't. I was in love with the romantic and ill-conceived idea that I could get her back. And how would I do that? Drunken late-night phone calls rife with begging and tears. Bravo! How hot is that? Sooooo not hot, and not the least bit effective, either. Not only was I dragging my heart through the muck, but also my dignity. I had managed to degrade myself even further—from someone she wasn't in love with anymore to someone she pitied and avoided. Now, to be fair, this particular girl was patient and tolerant with me, but I was making life miserable for her. I began to alienate my good friends with my obsession, my work began to suffer, and I looked like shit. Even worse, I was drinking like it was the day before Prohibition.

Well, one night after too many tequila shots I figured I would blow in a call to Ms. New York City just to see if there had been any change in her insistence that she was not the girl for me. (Here's where the story gets good.) She was living in the New York Paramount Hotel at the time, waiting for her apartment to open up. With the number committed to memory, I drunk-dialed . . . "Paramount Hotel," said the fellow on the other end. Now realize this: It's probably 2:30 A.M. Los Angeles time, making it 5:30 A.M. in New York. I don't know the exact time because numbers weren't making sense. Good start. So the desk clerk answers, "Paramount Hotel. How may I direct your call?" Well, I was so smashed that I couldn't even pronounce my lady's name. Seriously, I'd have made more sense if I'd just barked like a dog. The desk clerk said, "I'm sorry, sir, can you say that again?" I tried again, unsuccessfully. "Sir, perhaps you'd like to spell it?" (Oh my God, man! Have some self-respect. Put down the phone,

Greg!) But I didn't. I took a stab at spelling it. Finally, he under-
stood whom it was that I was trying to reach. But right before
he was about to put me through to her room he said the most
amazing thing. He said, "Are you sure you want to make this call,
sir?" What? I thought. Are you kidding me? Out of the drunken
blackness came this anonymous voice of concern. "Am I sure I
want to make this call?" And I had a moment. No, I thought, I
don't want to make this call. I've made this call before. This call
never works out. This call always makes it worse. This call takes
me further and further away from the place I want to be. Which
is a place that is dignified and cool. "No," I said. "I don't want
to make this call. Thanks." And I hung up and passed out, fully
clothed, the last shreds of my dignity still intact.

The next day, hungover and sad, I remembered the voice on
the other end of the line. The voice that had said, "Are you sure
you want to make this call?" I thought, Wouldn't it be great if
you had that voice in your head all the time? Your own personal
breakup buddy, someone there to make sure you don't make the
bad phone call, the ill-advised drive-by, the decision to dress up
in their clothes and pretend you're them as a way of getting
inside their thoughts? That's why we've come up with this book.
This book is that voice. We are the friends who care enough
about you to make sure you do this thing right. Breakups hurt
like a motherf*#ker, but they are not the end of the world. The
pain is temporary, and if handled properly, they can even be life-
changing. Our goal is to help you turn your breakup into the
event that changes your life for the better. After all . . . you are
a Superfox.

Greg

AMIIRA'S INTRO

It's past two in the morning. You're on your third glass of wine. You're wearing his sweater because it still smells like him (and quite frankly, he never really smelled that great, but I'm going to give it to you because I've been there). I've been the saddest girl in the world, with a mangled heart and the certainty that getting over him was impossible. I've been the girl so in love with a person incapable of giving me what I needed out of a relationship that I not only married him but gladly gave away every last shred of my self-esteem to keep him. I've been the girl who not only suffers through an unhealthy, demoralizing relationship but then goes back to it in hopes that time spent apart has inspired him to love me enough to change . . . or even try. And guess what? It didn't. I've been consumed with despair, confusion, anger—truly devastated by the end of a relationship that I thought was going to last forever. I've cried into glass after glass of pinot grigio, smoked packs of cigarettes, lost my appetite, my ability to sleep, and my ability to function. I've obsessed, rebounded, been pissed, sought professional help, leaned on my friends, moved across the country, got dogs, made new friends, shopped excessively, and even had other boyfriends who did love me despite the fact that I was still so hung up on the past that I was completely incapable of giving *them* what they needed from me. Truth be told, I rode that horse long after it had up and died and married someone else. On the outside, I wore the illusion that I was over it and that the end of the marriage was best for us both. But that charade was all smoke and mirrors and empty words. Being brokenhearted is like having broken ribs. On the outside it looks like nothing's wrong, but every breath hurts. Let's just say my ribs were broken for a long time.

Now, it may surprise you to hear that in all other areas of my life I was confident and successful. It's true. I had a kick-ass job, made good money, had lots of friends, a great apartment, cool clothes, excellent taste in music, etc. . . . But for whatever reason, getting over this guy took forever. He was my kryptonite. And like Superman, I was powerless in his wake. But if you've seen the movies, you know that Superman always figures out a way to overcome kryptonite. And thankfully, I did too.

Now, defeating kryptonite and getting over a broken heart is incredibly tough. It's also wildly empowering. But the even bigger victory is finally living your own life again without the constant presence of heartache. That's the goal, and we're here to help you get there. I've stood where you're standing now, broken to the point that I couldn't get past the idea that my life wasn't turning out the way I'd planned. But guess what? Once I got through it and started living my life differently, making better decisions and demanding more from myself and for myself, I got a windfall that I never imagined. Today, my life is even better than I ever dreamed or planned. I have a husband whom I adore and whose love and devotion for me blows my mind every day. I have two beautiful daughters who are the funniest and most delightful people I've ever had the joy of knowing. And I have the very best friends and family in the world, whom I am grateful for every day. I would have missed it all if I'd wasted my life trailing after my ex and staying stuck in my grief. It's like my Granny always said: "Even with all the mayonnaise in the world, you can't make chicken salad out of chicken shit." Feel free to apply that wisdom to your bad relationship.

Love,
Amiira

WHAT LIES AHEAD

o how is it that a Superfox like you finds herself holding the winning ticket in the pain lottery? A seemingly endless jackpot of sorrow that you won't be splitting with anyone else. That doesn't mean you're alone. In fact, as our stories show, everyone goes through it. But here's the thing that you need to know right now: YOU ARE GOING TO GET THROUGH THIS. And like every lottery winner, you can either take it in one lump sum and figure out what you're going to do with it, OR you can spread it out in yearly installments and really make it last. We prefer option one. Sure, it's less pain than if you drag it out for years, but if you take it all now, you get to decide what you're going to do with it. How to invest it, spend it, roll around in it—or get rid of it.

Breakups are among the most excruciating things that can happen to a person invited to the concert called life. We acknowledge this and in no way want to belittle your heartbreak.

But we've purposefully made the tone of this book humorous in an effort to distract you from the very real and overwhelming feelings that you're having. We intend to give you genuine advice and practical suggestions for not only dealing with this insufferable situation but also redecorating your living room. "What?" you ask. Believe it or not, it's all part of the process.

If you're reading our book right now, it's probably because you've been dumped, you're brokenhearted, you're still stuck on your ex, or even all of the above. Perhaps you were the dumper and are having second thoughts—we'll deal with you soon enough, but we're pretty sure you made the right decision. Whether you delivered or received the "It's Not You, It's Me" speech, as hard as it is to hear right now, your relationship wasn't a match. We know you wanted it to be and are hoping that we're going to tell you that this isn't real. That he or she will be knocking down your door tomorrow, begging to be taken back, and all your pain and heartache will be erased. That there's a simple way to fix all the problems, and if you just try a little bit harder you can still have the happily ever after that you envisioned. You want us to tell you that people *can* change—but the truth of the matter is that *it's called a breakup because it's broken*. Even if you can't see it right now, if you've broken up, at least one person in your relationship knows it deep down. And if he ended it, that means he doesn't want to try to fix it either.

The hard truth is that breakups are sink-or-swim. Some people spend their whole life in an emotional downward spiral because they can't get over lost love. Others, most notably you, use it as a turning point to reevaluate, rebuild, and possibly redecorate (we weren't kidding about the living room). Bottom line: This can be a breakup or a breakover. It's up to you.

"Who are you to give me advice?" you shout, disrupting the other customers in the bookstore. "Why should I listen to you guys or even read any further, for that matter?" Keep it down, Crazypants, everyone's looking at you now. Here's who we are. We're two people who have both experienced truly self-esteem-crushing, spirit-breaking, gut-wrenchingly painful breakups of which we were on the receiving end. Let's just say they were stinky and they also sucked and they made us want to lie in bed for the rest of our lives. Thank God we didn't make that choice. (Just think of the bedsores and long, curling fingernails we'd have by now.) Those breakups led to what we like to think of as our happy marriage. (Don't worry—you won't be hearing about our marriage every ten pages. There is nothing worse than self-satisfied married people telling you how it is. We just think it's significant that our worst experiences led to what we ultimately think of as best. 'Nuff said?)

This is a different book from *He's Just Not That Into You*. That book was designed specifically to help you figure out when your relationship was going nowhere or whether your boyfriend was, well, into you. But we know that even when you realize he's just not that into you, the hardest part can still be getting up the courage to end the relationship and move on. Breaking up is scary, painful, disruptive, and traumatic—even if you know on some level that it's the right thing to do—so *It's Called a Breakup Because It's Broken* is designed to help you *not only* get out of an unsatisfying relationship but also get over it so that you can be ready for the better things in life that are coming your way. At the end of the day, it's about whether YOU like yourself enough to face the reality that your romance wasn't working, to recognize that it wasn't giving you what you needed and deserved, and to pull yourself out of the dumps and seize the opportunity before you. Because as messed up as everything seems right now, this could be the single best thing that's ever happened to you.

That's right—even better than when you got your first apartment, found those Gucci stilettos on sale, won the Oscar for best actress, or whatever appears on your own personal highlight reel. Think about it this way: When you and your ex got into this relationship, you were two brand-new sports cars driving side by side. You were sleek, desirable, sexy, and confident, and the ride was exhilarating. After a while you zigged when he zagged, you weren't driving the same speed anymore, one of you was always trying to catch up, and eventually you crashed and totaled the cars. When the insurance paid out, one of you decided to buy a new car instead of fixing the totaled one. For those of you who don't own cars, the translation of this metaphor is that you and your ex (or soon-to-be ex) no longer share the belief that the relationship is worth fixing. One of you wants a new car altogether. And besides, who wants a relationship that despite attempted repairs always stalls when you try to shift gears? Not you.

It's called a breakup because it's broken, and in the pages ahead you will come to learn that that's actually a good thing. So read on, breakup warrior! From adversity comes greatness. Life's biggest rewards come from the biggest challenges, or something like that. Many of us have found the road to a better life and a truer love in the face of some serious heartbreak. Some of us even happened to have pens handy to write down catchy proverbs to help inspire or annoy you in your time of need. So let's dive in already, because there's nothing more annoying than a self-help book full of nothing but proverbs! We've done our best to make this book so much more.

The format includes a question-and-answer section, workbook exercises, firsthand stories from our own breakups, and a little thing we like to call the Psycho Confessional, which is where you can turn when you need an "At least I'm not doing that bad" boost to your self-esteem. The questions and examples in this book have come not only from our own experiences, but also from those of our friends and our extensive breakup survey, where well over 500 people shared the gory details of their sad but true breakups with us. You'll be glad they did. And now let's turn the page and start the process of finding our way back to an even more rocking you.

WHAT IF YOU'RE STILL TOGETHER?

*J*ust because you know that your relationship is no good doesn't make the process of ending it any easier. Even if you have reached the realization that he's just not that into you, you're just not that into him, or you're mutually not that into each other, that doesn't mean that you've been successful at pulling the trigger. We know that, and in fact have both been guilty of letting dead-end relationships linger on way past their shelf life because the task of ending them was just too difficult. It's hard to have the courage to walk away from the comfort of a relationship, even a bad one, and be alone for what may be a while. What's more, it's easy to find reasons not to end it: I don't want to have to look for another apartment, I don't have the money to be on my own, I won't have a date to my cousin's wedding, I can't stand the thought of him being with anyone else.

But here's the thing to remember: Wasting time in a relationship that blows is just that—wasted time. Time that could be spent looking for and meeting the person who's destined to be your perfect match. Ultimately, there's no benefit to hanging on—you're merely procrastinating and delaying the inevitable. Staying in a relationship that's on life support isn't going to bring it back to life. "But how will I get over it?" We'll help you get over it—that's what this book is all about. So do the *both* of you a favor and end it. Pick up the phone right now and tell him you need to talk. Pull the plug already and come with us on the road to the bigger, brighter future that awaits.

Part 1

THE BREAKUP

(Or, How the Hell Did a
Kick-Ass Lady Like Myself End Up
in This Agonizing Nightmare?)

INT. HIS APARTMENT—NIGHT
An attractive couple, late twenties, sit on the
couch in front of a burning fire. The setting is
romantic. He gets up and paces nervously, taking a swig from his bottle of beer.

                    HIM

        There's something I've been meaning to
        talk to you about.

She expectantly puts down her wineglass and
checks that her lips are appropriately glossed
for the big moment.

                    YOU

        We can talk about anything. That's why
        we're so perfect together.

He paces in front of her, searching for the right
words.

                    HIM

        It's just that . . . we've been together
        for a while now. And I always have a
        great time with you . . .

                    YOU

        I know, it's like we were made for each
        other!

                    HIM

     You're a really special person, and some-
     day you'll make the perfect wife . . .

                    YOU

     (excitedly) Yes???

He squats down in front of her and grabs both
her hands. She can hardly believe it's about to
happen . . .

                    HIM

     . . . Just not for me. I think we should
     see other people . . .

She clearly didn't hear him, as she interrupts
him . . .

                    YOU

     I'd love to! (realizing) Wait—what did
     you just ask me?

                    HIM

     (relieved) Really? That's great! I
     thought you were going to get really
     upset. I've been trying to figure out
     how to tell you that for weeks.

She gets up and walks to the kitchen and starts
pulling open all the drawers.

                    HIM

What are you looking for?

                    YOU

Something to hit you with.

Chapter One

IT'S CALLED A BREAKUP BECAUSE IT'S BROKEN

aAAAAAAAAAAAAAAAAAAAAAAAAAAAAAAA AAAAAHHHHHHH! F★#k, it hurts. It's rocking the very core of your being. You never saw it coming. You knew this was going to happen. You were going to do it first. You only broke it off with him before he broke it off with you. You guys were supposed to be together forever. You never liked him that much anyway. He was such a great kisser. The sex wasn't that great. You really liked his family. He hated your friends. You hated his shoes. You miss him soooooo much. There's no doubt about it—breakups suck. And now here you are holding this stupid "Breakup Book" because, quite honestly, you'd do anything not to feel like this and maybe this book will shed some light on what you're going through. Maybe you'll get some sleep tonight. Or stop sleeping all the time.

In these first few hours or days or weeks of your breakup,

there's one all-important truth that you need to recognize: Some things can't and shouldn't be fixed, especially that loser who dumped you or forced you to dump him. It's over for a reason, and even if you're in denial about it, deep down inside you probably know what that reason is. Even if you feel baffled by his decision to end it, it boils down to the same thing every time: Your relationship, despite its promise, has ceased to be right for one or both of you. It is, in effect, broken. That doesn't make the breakup any easier to handle or change the overwhelming nature of the sadness that you feel. But that sadness, in turn, doesn't make it less broken. If you've reached this point, where one or both of you feel that walking away is the best course of action, the cracks are there. And starting today, you're not the kind of woman who settles for broken or hangs on to damaged goods, be it a radio, a pair of shoes, or a relationship. Your life is not a yard sale. It's time to get rid of all the broken stuff that you've been lugging around for days, months, and maybe even years, and make the bold decision to start looking for stuff that works. The bright, clean, simple, easy, runs-so-smoothly-I-don't-even-have-to-think-about-it kind of works. Being the first one to recognize that a relationship isn't a match doesn't win you any great prize—just the guilt of having to hurt someone's feelings. So even though you are clearly wounded, getting out of this broken relationship is the best thing possible, even if you didn't know it was broken until now.

"But some things *can* be fixed," you say. True, but can your relationship be fixed? Anything is possible, but we'd say probably not. Generally, if one person thinks that the breakup is the right move, they're probably right even if it feels so wrong. Because unless there are two people putting on the coveralls and getting down in the trenches with some duct tape and superglue and a fierce determination, it isn't going to happen. Need more convincing? How about this: The person you loved took a good long look at the awesomeness that is you, evaluated your relationship together, and said, "No, thanks. I'll try my luck elsewhere." Or you said it to him. Either way, that alone should make you realize that it wasn't a match made in heaven and they're not worth donning coveralls for. Anyone who assesses you or your relationship as disposable is not worthy of your time or tears.

Right now, your mind is probably working overtime to come up with all the reasons that you should still be together. Your heart is hurting and your mind wants to find a way to undo the pain. Just remember, though, that any reasons you come up with are ultimately irrelevant. The harsh reality is that even if you have everything else in common, the one thing you don't have in common is the belief that this relationship can work. That, my friend, trumps your shared love of puppies, The Dave Matthews Band, and Mexican food.

It's hard not to rack your brain, searching for reasons why the two of you couldn't make it work, but sometimes the only real answer is the simplest one: People come together and move apart. It's the age-old ebb and flow of relationships. Some are shorter journeys, and others were meant for a lifetime. That goes for friendships as well. We become attached to what's familiar and sometimes we hold on to things that are safe and predictable even if they're bad for us. A lot of the pain you are experiencing right now is actually fear. Fear of things being different than how you liked them, fear of never finding another love, fear of being alone, fear of having to fill your time differently. We're afraid of the unknown. The answer to all the questions swirling in your head— What will I do on weekends? Will I meet someone else?—is "You won't know until you get there." That's hard, and it's scary. But for the moment, you need to concentrate on what you do know—that you and he no longer share the belief that your relationship has a future. It's broken, and the longer you stay stuck in a dead-end relationship or spend your days mourning one, the less time you get on this planet to experience a great one.

So take a deep breath, steel yourself, and realize that this is going to hurt for a while. There is no quick remedy for the powerful sting of heartbreak, though we're going to try to make it easier for you throughout the book. You're going to feel like crap head to toe and run the gamut of emotions. Edgy, moody, angry, depressed, nauseated—you name it. In fact, the amount of time it takes for you to start feeling great about yourself again is directly proportional to how much it sucks right now—especially if you weren't the one who broke it off. Because at the end of the day, someone you loved, trusted, and valued has rejected you, and that really smarts. It's hard to not take it personally. But— and here's the important part—the fact of the matter is, they're wrong about you. Just because your relationship is broken doesn't mean you are! No matter what happened between you, no matter what you may or may not have done wrong, you are still a kick-ass person. And even though you might not believe it right now, this breakup is the first step toward finding someone truly worthy of your greatness.

But Greg, I've Got Questions

But how can a relationship just break with no warning?

Dear Greg

My boyfriend and I have been together for three years and have always had the perfect relationship. We moved in together last year and he started talking about getting married, having kids, the whole deal. He even took me to look at engagement rings a few weeks before Christmas, so naturally I assumed what would be under the Christmas tree for me. Since I thought I was getting an engagement ring, I maxed out my credit card to buy him a plasma TV for Christmas. Well, Christmas morning comes and he was shocked when he opened the plasma TV. But that was nothing compared to the shock when I opened his gift—a cashmere sweater and a necklace! What? Then, the next day, he tells me he's not sure "I'm the one" and he thinks I should move out and we should take a break so he can figure some things out!! Now he's got the apartment and the plasma TV that I'll be paying off for the rest of my life. I've tried to remind him of how good we were together and that getting married was his idea, but he just keeps apologizing and telling me he needs time apart. How can somebody go from wanting to marry you to not even wanting to talk to you for no reason? What can I do to make him realize that we should be together?

Please write back.

Marla

Dear Plasma Giver,

First of all, never buy a man a plasma TV until you're married. (My grandmother used to say that.) A lot of men think once they have a plasma TV they don't need a girlfriend. Sounds like your boyfriend's one of them. The truth is that if he's going to come to the conclusion that you guys should be together, he's going do it on his own. There's nothing you can do to make him want to be with you, and more important, want to marry you. One of the suckiest and most frustrating facts of life is that sometimes relationships just end, often without reason. I truly believe that sometimes both men and women simply run out of love, even when there was a lot of it in the beginning. What blows even more is that you were completely blindsided—even though the relationship was broken on his end, he had clearly led you to believe you were in the same place emotionally. What a shitty new reality for you to get your head around now. But the sooner you do, the sooner you can get your head around this great new thought: HEY, SUPERFOX, YOU ARE HEADED SOMEWHERE FABULOUS AND THERE ARE GREAT POSSIBILITIES AHEAD. You should also let him know that the proper etiquette is that if a girl breaks off an engagement she should give back the ring. If a man breaks up with you, he should give back the TV.

> But why didn't he just break up with me
> instead of making me do it?

Dear Greg

I've been seeing this guy for about eight months. At first we were just hooking up, but then we started really dat-

ing, exclusively. We were practically living at each other's houses, rarely spending even one night apart. He even gave me a drawer at his place and a toothbrush! So a few weeks ago he started acting weird, and I asked if something was wrong. He said that things had moved along faster than he'd anticipated, and that even though it freaked him out, he was really happy with the way things were going and cared about me more than he'd expected to. I thought, Great! Then he's suddenly too tired to come over or has to get up early the next day so he doesn't think I should spend the night. So we went back to only seeing each other a few nights a week. Not great. When he got really distant, I knew something was up, so I checked his e-mails on his Sidekick when he was in the bathroom. It was clear from all the e-mails between him and TamiLynn78 that he'd been seeing someone else. So I confronted him about it and he didn't deny it, so I told him we were O.V.E.R. and stormed out of his apartment. Now, this is the part where he was supposed to come running after me—but he didn't! He just let me go, and I haven't heard from him since. What's up with that? I really want him to want me back and feel remorse for hurting me. Is that too much to ask?
Linda

Dear Yes It Is Too Much to Ask,
First of all, I think it's great you checked his e-mails instead of talking to him. Sounds like you had a great, open, trusting relationship in which you dug around in his personal business while he cheated on you. Why did it have to end? I'm going to say this and

it's going to suck (but understand where I'm coming from). He broke up with you months ago and let you do the dirty work. It's a weird, passive-aggressive trick that men have perfected for centuries. Chances are he didn't want to hurt your feelings, so he behaved in a way that would make you break up with him. I call this the "Backhanded Breakup." Men (and women) have done it for years. Not only that, but he had an escape plan involving another bed to crash on. What a scumbag! I'm sure he's getting right on that remorse you were hoping for. The only thing he has done right is not contact you. You should gladly accept this radio silence because your relationship has been broken for a while, and get on with your grieving because you are moving on to something better.

But how do you know we're not going to get back together?

Dear Greg

My boyfriend of three years and I decided to move in together about a month ago. In fact, it was his idea. Since he had the bigger place, we agreed that I'd let go of my apartment and move in with him. Everything was perfect—we repainted in colors that we both liked and started figuring out what pieces of furniture we'd keep when we merged our stuff. Then, the day before I'm supposed to move, after I've already given notice at my apartment and it's been rented, he tells me that he's done some thinking and that I'm not "the one." He thinks that living together is a mistake and a waste of time for the both of us because

it only delays us "finding our destinies." He's an amazing
person that I can't imagine living without, and I know that
if he's given a little more time he'll realize that we are each
other's destiny. Great guys aren't a dime a dozen. And he
obviously has really strong feelings for me if he wanted us
to live together a few weeks ago! Don't you think I should
be patient with him if I really believe that we're meant to
be together?
Clarissa

Dear Destiny's Child,
Maybe you huffed too many paint fumes, but he said the words you
are "not the one." That's pretty conclusive as far as these things
go, and despite the really awful timing, you've got to admire the
guy's honesty. He did it to save you both more time and pain down
the line. You don't have to like it, you don't have to enjoy it, but
you do need to hear it. I know this hurts like a motherf*#ker, but
it's going to keep hurting if you don't accept that it's over. Plus
he used the word "destiny." What kind of New Age bullshit is that?
People like to think they can control their destiny, but I think des-
tiny is listening and seeing what's really happening and then mak-
ing the smart, albeit sometimes painful, decision to move forward
without another person. If you guys are meant to be together, I'm
sure his third eye will let him know and then he'll surely move
mountains to win you back. But I know for a fact that waiting for
someone who may not be coming and being in pain are not your
destiny. So realize that it's called a breakup because it's broken—
and move on.

But what if our relationship really was great?

Dear Greg

Here's one for you. I went out with a great guy for two years. He didn't cheat, never lied, always made me feel special, and basically treated me like a queen. Then, two months ago, he tells me that he doesn't have feelings for me anymore and doesn't see the relationship going any further and hopes that we can be friends. I know for a fact that there's not another woman, so I can only take him at his word because he's never been anything but up front with me. So what happened?

Jennifer

Dear Great Gatsby,

Some guys (and ladies too) are great. In fact, many of them are. That's why we like them so much, fall in love with them, and are disappointed when it doesn't work out in the end. Sadly, that's how it is sometimes. Two people in a relationship either grow together or apart over time. Sometimes they do both, and that's the most puzzling. Regardless, it's a very real occurrence that one's feelings can stop growing for no identifiable reason. What you can be grateful for is his honesty, the untarnished memory of a healthy relationship, and the realization that great guys do exist, and hopefully you'll find the right one for you that you'll go the distance with. You found one once, you'll find one again. Promise.

But why does it still hurt?

Dear Greg

My boyfriend and I broke up almost a year ago and it still hurts! We were only together for a year and a half, so shouldn't I be over this? They say it takes half the time of the total length of the relationship to get over it, but that equation hasn't worked for me. I swear it hurts as much today as it did a year ago. I still think about him every day and think of all the great memories we had together, and it makes me so mad that he just threw that all away. How long is it going to hurt and how do I get over this?
Lauren

Dear Time Stands Still,
I do believe that someone did say that it takes half the time of a relationship to get over it. There's another formula, though, that may be more accurate; if your pet hamster dies, you count the number of years it was alive, divide that by its number of paws, and find the square root. OR maybe *mathematical equations do not apply to the heart.* I think the time it takes to feel better about a breakup, Hot Stuff, is directly proportional to the time it takes to feel better about yourself. When you feel bad about yourself, you replay loops in your head. You replay great moments you guys had together so you can reassure yourself that you "blew it." You go back over mistakes you made: "If only I'd been skinny, sexy, whatever" to "What about that time I set his car on fire . . ." (Uh, okay, some things may have been a factor.) So you sit around and devalue yourself. You think about what you could have said or

should have done—or what you might say if he comes crawling back—instead of being present in the moment and working toward a new and better future. It's called a breakup because it's broken. It can't be fixed, so you have to let it go, and only then will your pain begin to subside. The hard part about time is that it actually takes time. Sorry.

THE *Best* WORST NEWS

The best worst news is that you're broken up. You're in the thick of it. There's no more dreading when or if it's going to happen, or how badly you're going to feel. You're here, and like everything else in life, the reality is never quite as bad as you feared it would be. You didn't die, the world didn't end, food still tastes decent, and now you have time to reconnect with friends, catch up on your reading, and hog the bed all to yourself if nothing else.

The super sucky hard part is adjusting to this new reality and, of course, going through some real heartache. The thing about breakups and the pain that accompanies them is that they can't just be undone or get better. Even the most mutual of splits usually hurts one party more than the other and can lead to an avalanche of emotions that takes some time to clear. But the flip side of breaking up—and here's the Best News part—is that you are also breaking *free* from a relationship that wasn't working. Freedom means no more agonizing, no more drama, and no more time wasted on someone who wasn't appreciative of who you really are. Freedom means you can redesign your life and the sky's the limit—you can take all the things you hoped for in your relationship, all your dreams about what love should be and feel and look like, and find a guy who will actually make them happen. During this time when you feel decimated and powerless, remember that you are still in control of at least one thing—yourself. And while you can't make someone take back a breakup, you do get a say in what happens next. You get to decide whether to use this situation as a turning point, and be dignified in your grief, or let it overtake you and hold you back. So start now. Start today. Don't be a victim of heartbreak, be a take-charge superstar! (Yeah, that's kind of goofy, but you know what we mean.)

WHAT I DID WRONG BY GREG

It happened slowly and it super sucked. She'd been hanging out with this guy from work—let's call him DUDE. You know, going out and having a drink, that kind of thing. Just her and the Dude, who is really good-looking. A lot of people are handsome. And funny. A lot of people are handsome and funny. Totally cool. Then I caught them making out on our driveway and I thought, "This is suspicious." But she was probably just helping him get something out of his mouth with her tongue. She was kind like that. Soon thereafter, she lost interest in sleeping with me and even moved into a hotel for a while. Still, she insisted I was her boyfriend, and I thought, "Great." Then one day she calls me to say she's buying a place in New York. "New York? But you live and work in Los Angeles!" "I know, but I hate it here." "But I'm here." "You could come to New York." "And do what?" Silence. I hung up. When your girlfriend moves to a different city, there are really some cracks in the foundation of your relationship. It dawned on me I might be losing her. I had to concoct a plan, some way to get her not to move. Something dramatic. Isn't that what they do in the movies? Drama? You know, stand on the lawn with a boom box, that kind of thing. Seriously, if I could have crashed through her hotel window on the end of a golden rope dressed like a pirate holding a boom box, I would have. The problem with being the guy with the boom box is that in the movie he's the hero but in real life he gets carted away by the cops. Scratch the pirate getup. So I decided to break up with her as a way to get her back. How could this go wrong? I'll break up with her, she'll realize the huge mistake she's making, and she'll call off the move to New York. I mean, what's in New York? It's just a bunch of tall buildings and . . . that DUDE . . . Oh shit!

But here's what's worse: Even when I added it all up—The Driveway, The Hotel, New York, and Dude—I still had *HOPE!!* And why wouldn't I? She was making out with Dude, living in a Hotel, and moving to New York. What's not to be hopeful about? Who thinks that? A sane person looks at what's going on, makes an assessment, and then moves in the direction that is the least painful. But when you're hurting, you are not sane, and for whatever reason, often only interested in more pain. So I broke up with her. To which she said, "Great." So I then asked her to take me back. Oh wow! Now I was giving her another chance to reject me on top of the rest, and guess what . . . I still wouldn't let it go. Quite often I think back to this event and wonder why I didn't just say to her, "Hey, it sucks, but you don't seem to be into me, and since you won't break up with me, I'm gonna do it." And then walk away quietly with dignity instead of indulging in the behavior outlined in the pages to come. If you are where I was then right now, know that you can walk away with your dignity today. Trust me, please. You will wish you had.

How I Got Through It   by Amiira

At some point you realize that you're not going to die from a broken heart—though you'll surely contemplate the feasibility of it for a while. Believe me, you'll get there at your own pace—hopefully, sooner rather than later. For me it took years of on again/off again before I finally was able to really understand that he just wasn't that into me. It was years of big promises with no follow-through. Lots of pushing me away just to reel me back in the moment before I was out the door. In retrospect, I'm embarrassed by how little effort on his part it took for me to come back or stay. I was so desperate for him to love me, to want me, to fight for me that I was literally grateful for any mere scrap of effort. I'd made so many excuses for his inability to treat me well that even the smallest gesture was amplified in my head. After years of this, I finally got my head out of my ass and realized that aside from feeling insecure and fragile about the state of my relationship all the time, we also wanted entirely different things out of life! (Even the brightest of girls aren't above pulling the wool over their own eyes in the name of hope.) Having a moment of clarity like that is worth your entire kingdom. The liberation of recognizing that you can stand up for yourself and demand action is incredible. And that's what I did. I sat him down and told him that he was wasting my time.

By not committing to either working on the issues we were having or to NOT working on them, he was keeping me in a kind of relationship purgatory, and I was over it. So I gave him the option—you can choose to work on it or choose to NOT work on it. No hard feelings. I proposed it as a choice because by this point I wasn't angry, I just wanted to know. I needed an answer so that another few years of my life wouldn't be wasted with empty promises. He said he couldn't make a decision right then and asked for some time. I gave him four weeks (which was really quite generous, considering he had already given me the answer—but I was doing the best I could). So four weeks later I asked him again, and he said he still didn't know. (Clearly, he had put about as much thought into this as every other aspect of our relationship.) Well, that's an answer, right? Not caring enough to even think about it seems like an answer, doesn't it? If you wanted to be with me, it would cross your mind to think about it. If you wanted to be with me, you'd do whatever it took to make it work. If you wanted to be with me, you'd know. *You'd know.* For years I thought "I don't know" and "I don't know if I can" were words that meant what they said. But from that moment on I knew . . . "I don't know" means NO! "I don't know" means I'm too cowardly to tell you the truth because I can't deal with confrontation. "I don't know" means please do the dirty work for me because I don't want to hurt your feelings even more than I already have. Sure I was sad. I had married this person. Planned on spending my life with him. That moment sucked all the air out of my lungs and filled my head with white noise. But it was also the moment I knew that it was time to take care of me. We decided to split up, and in retrospect I think he had been hoping this moment would come for a long time. I think he had been trying to get me to break up with him forever by his actions—but my hope had blinded me.

Now, I was incredibly lucky to be able to afford what I did next. I called my best friend in Los Angeles, told her what happened, and booked a ticket on the next flight there. I spent a week away from my life, from him, from the hard stuff. I drank, I smoked, I cried, I watched sad movies, I slept, I flirted with other boys, and I distracted myself. After a week, I returned to reality and the heaviness that was in my heart. When a marriage or any significant relationship collapses, the sadness and grief can be overwhelming. In the midst of all this heartache and pain, you have to comprehend and adjust to the idea that your whole universe has been upended, even when you know it's the right thing. Going through a breakup is awful. It's a full-body experience. Every nerve ending feels it constantly, and every second feels like an eternity in your head.

So how'd I get through it? Well, the night he moved out, two of my best friends came over for dinner so that I wouldn't be alone. I hardly ate, but we downed a bottle of wine. Another friend of mine called to check in, and when I burst into tears she hopped in a cab, came over, and spent the night so the bed wouldn't be so big and I wouldn't have to be alone. She made sure I got out of the house and went to work the next day, and she offered to stay with me until I didn't need her to. I allowed myself to lean on my friends immediately, and they rallied around me. Their strength and love made me strong enough to endure some seriously shitty times.

AWESOME THOUGHT That annoying thing that your ex did will never bother you again.

Journeywork Workbook and Sometimes Cookbook

Crossword Puzzle

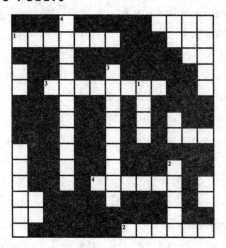

Across

1. Your ex is an _____ (7 letters)
2. What he did was totally _____ (6 letters)
3. You are a _____ (8 letters)
4. You deserve _____ (6 letters)

Down

1. Take the "L" out of Lover and it's _____ (4 letters)
2. If it doesn't kill you it makes you _____ (5 letters)
3. Breakup – up + Over = _____ (9 letters)
4. You are going to get _____ _____ (2 words - 11 letters)
   (also the name of Hole's breakthrough record *Live* _____
   _____)

Answers:

Across
1. ASSHOLE
2. F*#KED
3. SUPERFOX
4. BETTER

Down
1. OVER
2. DRINK
3. BREAKOVER
4. THROUGH THIS

PSYCHO CONFESSIONAL

After he broke up with me, I told him that we needed to go for a drive to talk. While driving, I did the usual, crazy breakup talk, threw around some profanities, told him he had wasted my time, and so on. I told him I'd still like to be friends and see if we couldn't fix what was wrong with our relationship. He told me he didn't think that was a good idea. He thought we needed to separate completely. I believe the quote was, "It's not you, it's me. I can't fix the fact that I don't feel that way about you anymore." How original. I continued to drive ten miles out of town (imagine farms, vast empty fields, you get the idea). He started to get a little suspicious and asked if we could start heading back. I said no and continued to drive. After five minutes of silence, I pulled over and said, "Here's your stop." He got out, I threw the batch of cookies I had recently made for him at him, shouted a few obscenities, and said, "There, now we are separated completely and I can't fix the fact that I don't feel like driving you home anymore." I must mention that, after dumping his ass by the side of the road, five minutes later it started pouring and the tornado sirens started to go off. No wonder he turned every shade of white and sheepishly avoided eye contact with me when I ran into him a year later!

Anonymous
Raleigh, NC

EXT. CHICAGO STREET—DAY
Estella, an attractive forty-year-old business-woman, walks down a busy street talking assertively into her cell phone. She is talking to a representative at her wireless company.

                REPRESENTATIVE (V.O.)

    Fool Proof Wireless. How can we assist
    you today?

                ESTELLA

    Yes, I seem to be having some problems
    with my cell phone.

                REPRESENTATIVE (V.O.)

    What sort of problems?

                ESTELLA

    Well, my voice mail doesn't seem to
    work. I haven't had any messages for a
    week.

                REPRESENTATIVE (V.O.)

    Are you able to make outgoing calls?

                ESTELLA

    Well, yes . . . but I'm pretty sure
    that my text messages aren't working,
    because when I send one . . .

                REPRESENTATIVE (V.O.)

It goes unanswered?

                    ESTELLA

(relieved) Yes. And I don't seem to be
getting any incoming calls.

                REPRESENTATIVE (V.O.)

Let me just check out the line for you.

                    ESTELLA

Thank you so much. (PAUSE) It's just
that my parents are older and they
might need to reach me if there's an
emergency or something . . .

                REPRESENTATIVE (V.O.)

Hang on—I think I see the problem . . .
He's not coming back.

Chapter Two

THERE ARE NO
NEW MESSAGES

What did heartbroken people do before phones? Come home and stare at the mailbox? Stand in their driveway and wait for the stagecoach? Run to the Western Union to see if anyone had Morse Coded them? Stare into the sky waiting for the messenger pigeon? The phone is clearly one of the best inventions of all time, but it is also the most lethal of weapons during a breakup. It mocks you when it's silent, it beckons to you when you're drunk, and it's only too glad to tell you, "You have no new messages." It is, in fact, the barometer by which we take the temperature of our broken heart. If we didn't have to live in today's modern world, I would advise you to get rid of yours now. Because what you need to do above all else is have some distance from the person who is causing your pain. Even if it's the last thing you want, it's the thing you need the most. Self-imposed distance will expedite your recovery more than anything else you do for yourself. Not the kind where you go live in a cave and eat moss—healthy distance.

The first rule of the smart girl's breakup is NO CALLING! This will be expanded on later, in the Breakover section of the book, but it doesn't take a lot of detective work to figure out why. But here's the main reason that people usually overlook: He doesn't want you to call. (In fact, write that down and put it by your phone.) He broke up with you for a reason, and good or bad, he doesn't want to hear from you right now. Even if he said "Call me" during your final conversation. He probably only did so to ease his guilt about breaking up with you. And if you broke up with him, leave him alone already! Harsh, we know, but drum it into your head before you dial—even if you both intend on being friends down the line. The same goes for text messaging, instant messaging, BlackBerrying, blueberrying, or any other form of communication. Actions speak louder than words, and calling him doesn't say, "I'm cool with this whole breakup thing and just wanted to see what was going on because I'm a mature adult"— it says, "I still need your approval and am lost without you." And we know that isn't the message you want to send him.

Speaking of messages, here's Rule #2: Don't check his. EVER. First, it's illegal; second, it makes you seem crazy; and third, anything you find out will only make it worse or confirm your worst fears. It's like heaping pain on top of pain. So save yourself the indignity of being the kind of person who breaks into his voice mail, e-mail, snail mail, whatever, and just assume the worst: He's dating someone else and it's Heidi Klum. Then start dealing with it.

Don't get us wrong; we understand the need for contact, communication, and information during this shitty time. We all go through a kind of withdrawal when we suddenly lose someone we cared about from our lives, and any glimmer of those things can be a beacon in your darkness. But again, it's like trying to get sober and allowing yourself just a sip to get you through the day. Indulging in the need rather than being strong enough to overcome it will keep you both addicted to your ex and immobile, stuck in your breakup angst. One of the keys to getting through this time is to keep yourself in motion and not allow yourself to sit around wallowing. We hate to sound like high school coaches, but you've got to walk it off, sport! Tormenting yourself with the phone—worrying that you missed a voice mail, jumping up hopefully every time it rings—is not your ex's fault, it's something you are doing to yourself, and you need to recognize that. Take a moment and get real with yourself about why you're doing what you're doing. Does it really make you feel better to call his cell and then wonder what he's doing when he doesn't answer? Do you feel empowered reading his e-mails and learning that his life is going on full steam without you? We think not. And if you're honest with yourself, you'll agree. In addition to the legitimate pain you are experiencing from having been rejected, hurt, and disappointed, you are picking at the scabs. (Eew!) None of these activities befit the strong, sexy, totally self-possessed Superfox we know you want to be.

In nearly half of the breakup surveys that we received, making compulsive phone calls, drunk dialing, obsessively checking messages, and breaking into an ex's voice mails were among the biggest regrets that people had. Interestingly, nearly all of them admitted that they actually felt worse when they did these things, yet they were unable to control their impulse or need to do so. That says a lot about the commonality of how heartbreak affects us, and how we can be our own worst enemies in times of need. The big lesson here is that when it comes to your ex, any urge or impulse to contact him will do more harm than good, and you need to fight these urges however you can.

A few brave, superhuman souls inspired us with their stories, and we hope they do the same for you. One woman wrote to us that she threw away the SIM card from her cell phone so that she couldn't check her messages because it was driving her crazy. Another guy wrote to us that he paid a friend $300 to travel with him at all times so he wouldn't call his ex. One lady asked her neighbor to take her phones out of her apartment every night and return them in the morning so that she wouldn't be tempted. Now, these could be considered extreme measures, but when you really think about them, they're actually pretty smart. These people recognized that they were powerless over the phone and their own obsession, and took action. Getting a new cell phone card, hiring a babysitter, and getting the phones out of the house during your weakest hours is basic self-preservation. More than that, it's empowering! These people didn't die from it and weren't wildly inconvenienced—rather, the lack of phone contact allowed them to maintain their dignity when they felt it slipping away. They are role models for the brokenhearted!

Just think, before you dial that number again, how great you'll feel a year from now if you can look back on yourself and not feel embarrassed, defeated, or pathetic. Because you know that a year from now this pain will be a distant memory and not the open sore it is today. Ask yourself: "Do I really want to make this call?" You have the opportunity to be bigger than you are right at this very moment. So don't be afraid to ask for help. Your friends and family love you and want you to get through this feeling stronger rather than broken. Keep a list by the phone of people you can call *instead* of him. Just dial them up and say, "I'm calling you instead." Your friends will understand and help you through this—chances are they've been there too.

Above all, remember that every step of this process is an opportunity to take care of and honor yourself. Every moment of pain, weakness, and discomfort puts you in a position to choose how you will react and how you will alleviate your condition. Calling him doesn't make it better—it only pulls you back into the cycle of heartbreak. He is the past. You are the future.

Write these down and keep them with you at all times:

Alcohol + Phone = Danger.
Alcohol + Text Messenger = Danger.
Alcohol + Phone Camera = All over the Internet!

But Greg, I've Got Questions

But what if he can't tell that it's me calling?

Dear Greg

My number shows up as "Private" on caller ID, so even if I call a thousand times he can never prove that it's me. Sometimes I just need to know that he's home and not out with another girl, and it's not like he can STAR-69 me because I have that blocked. Is that so bad?

Jamie

Dear Caller ID,
You've been eating denial by the bowl for breakfast if you think for a nanosecond that he doesn't KNOW it's you calling him all the time. And your actions are only confirming his belief that you shouldn't be together. Is that so bad? you ask. Ask yourself this: How does it make you feel to be spending your hours, days, weeks, or months not living your life because you're pretending to be a telemarketer? Hey, Saucy Girl, by stepping away from the phone you're taking the first step toward living your life.

But he said to call.

Dear Greg

When we broke up, he said to "keep in touch and let me know how you're doing." So I know that he's worried about me and still cares about me even if we're not together anymore. Don't you think that keeping the lines of communication open will make him realize that he misses me sooner than if we didn't talk at all?
Lindsay

Dear Communicado,
He said that because saying, "Well, I'm never going to see you again ever" would have been awkward. "Hey, let's never speak again" or "I don't want to know how you are" won't get him out of the breakup conversation as easily. Let's let him know how you're doing by NOT calling him. Quite honestly, he'll be more intrigued by the fact that you didn't call than if you did. Not keeping the lines of communication open says a lot about somebody.

It says they've moved on and are not interested in spending their valuable time on someone who doesn't want to be with them. Here's the truth: "Keep in touch and let me know how you're doing" doesn't actually mean that. The real translation is "I feel bad about this and hope you'll be okay, but I'm moving on." And therefore, so should you.

But what if I have a legitimate reason?

Dear Greg

I can't stop calling my ex-boyfriend. I have a valid reason because I still have some of his stuff. Not that it's the most valuable stuff in the world, but I have one of his favorite jackets, so it's not like he doesn't care about it. When we do talk, he's really nice at first and we have a great conversation. He's even admitted to thinking about me, but he never wants to get together so I can give him his things. He keeps telling me to just mail them or leave them outside in a box, but I don't want them to get stolen or lost in the mail. If he didn't want me to call, don't you think he'd just say so?

Joanna

Dear Box Full of Excuses,
Maybe what he's really saying is that he wants you to mail *yourself* to him in a box. If you're going to twist words around, why not really go for it? Stop calling your ex-boyfriend. Having his stuff is not really a valid reason to call, it's an excuse. And every time you use this excuse, he lets you know that he wants his stuff back but

doesn't want to see you. Now, you can make excuses as to why that is, too. Perhaps he's afraid that seeing you will trigger an avalanche of emotions that he can't handle and he'll fling himself into your arms . . . but we both know that's not true. The bottom line is, he doesn't want to see you. That sucks. It hurts. And every call you make is just asking him to reject you again. Take his stuff, put it on his porch—or better yet, put it on your porch and give it to the garbageman so you can finally be rid of that box of excuses to call him.

But what if he calls me?

Dear Greg

I've been so good about not calling my ex. But the thing is, he calls me every time he's been out drinking and wants to talk. I'm still totally in love with him and don't want to not take his calls, but even when I tell him I can't talk to him, he doesn't take no for an answer. He just shows up at my door, tells me he misses me and made a huge mistake. Then one thing leads to another and we end up sleeping together and he's gone the next day. I know he's just using me for a booty call, but I can't help myself. What do I do? I don't want to have to change my number—what if he needs to get ahold of me in an emergency?
Dawn

Dawn, Dawn, Dawn, Dawn,
He's basically saying, "I really love you on Friday from 2 A.M. to 3 A.M. A lot. Seriously." You know what dawns on me? That you

deserve someone who wants to be with you all the time, not just when he's drunk and looking to get laid. I applaud the first part of your letter where you say you've been good about not calling. That's a hard thing to do, and I don't mean to belittle it when I say that taking his drunk phone calls and letting him manipulate you for sex is like taking one step forward and sixteen steps back. I'm sure the drunk booty call isn't indicative of the loving relationship you once had, so at this point you're just taking scraps from someone who has relieved himself of any emotional attachment or responsibility to you. Block his number or change yours. And tell him to take you off of his "in case of emergency contact information sheet." By the way . . . sex is not an emergency.

But what if I can't stop breaking into his IM account?

Dear Greg

I know my ex-boyfriend's password to his instant messenger account. I had the feeling he was seeing a new girl, so I signed on as him (ThePantyMan) and started talking to the girl I had this feeling about (Sarah8476). I asked her if she had fun last night, and where she thought we (they) were headed in their relationship. When she said she'd like to seriously date him, I said, "That won't be possible. I'm still in love with my ex-girlfriend, you and I are just sex. It's really all you're good for." She signed off. It felt so good to have put an end to that! But now I can't stop. I go on all the time and talk to girls just to make sure they aren't seeing him, and if I sense they are acting flirtatious

*I say something ridiculous to make sure they never talk to
him again.*
Zoë

Dear IM a Mess,
I've got a game you can play—how about pretending not to be
completely crazy? Really, what has happened to you? The Panty
Man has moved on, or at least he's trying to, and eventually he'll
meet someone who sticks despite his stupid online name and your
sneaky ways. I think it's time you took a good look at the person
you've become and realize that you've bottomed out. Sabotaging
your ex's love life won't change the FACT that he doesn't want to
be with you. It only reduces you to a kind of behavior that can't
possibly make you feel good about who you are, because it's
pathetic. And I'd bet pathetic isn't what you were shooting for in
your childhood dreams. Put your computer in the closet, go out-
side, and get some fresh air into that mixed-up head of yours.

But I'm used to talking to him
all the time.

Dear Greg

I was only dating my ex a few months when we broke up, but
in that time we fell in love and did everything together. Now
that we're broken up, I can't stop thinking about him.
Everything reminds me of him. Whenever something hap-
pens that makes me think of him (which is all the time), I
want to call him, or e-mail him, or IM him. He's nice about
it, but then when he tells me he has to go I feel let down.

How do I break this addiction? I know I shouldn't talk to him at all, but I just can't quit cold turkey. This is killing me.
Scarlett

Dear Killing Me Softly,
That's what breakups feel like. I don't mean to be a hard-ass, but if they didn't there would be no need for this book. And you *can* go cold turkey and you should, because the sooner you do, the sooner the pain will subside. It's not like you are being asked to dismantle a nuclear bomb; this is something that you can do. Plus, even if he's civil, he really doesn't want to hear from you. It's as simple as this: Call a girlfriend instead. Share your life with someone who cares about you. Take it one day at a time, and whenever you make it through, do something nice for yourself as a reward.

But what if we were best friends?

Dear Greg

My best friend Brian let me know one night after too many tequila shots that he was in love with me. Understand that this was my best friend—not just my best guy friend—for the last seven years. At first I was unsure about taking our relationship to another level, but then I decided that there was no one I'd rather be with and we jumped in with both feet. Things were great for the first few months, and I thought, "Wow! I'm going to end up marrying my best friend." Well, a few months after that he decided we were better as friends after all and wanted to go back to how things were. I was devastated! I truly fell in love with him

and now can't just go back to being his friend. I would lit-
erally die if he started telling me about dating other girls
the way he did before this all started. I told him I couldn't
be his friend, at least not for a while—but now I'm going
through the most painful breakup of my life because I've
lost my boyfriend and, more importantly, my closest con-
fidant—the person I shared everything with! It's so hard
not to reach out to him! How do you get through something
like this without your best friend?
Jackie

Dear BFF,
Meet your new best friend. It's you. And your new best friend (who
looks exactly like you) wants you to know that while people always
want to be friends after they split up, it is virtually impossible. I
could be wrong, but a best friend isn't someone who makes you feel
horrible and sad every time you see him. So don't do it. It's like
making an alcoholic dry out in a bar. It's hard, unfair, and will only
make your pain last longer because you won't have any distance
from it. Remember, life is long, and if you were meant to be friends
you will be eventually, but not today. This is crucial: The sooner you
stop calling him or spending time with him and work on healing your-
self, the sooner the time will come when you can really be his friend
(though by then you may not even want to). This is what you have
other friends and your family for. And while a broken heart is a bro-
ken heart, there's something to be said for the empathy of friends
of the same sex who've been there. This is because men and women
experience things differently and offer support in different ways.

And since your best guy friend has been cut from the team, it seems like an excellent time to let your girlfriends take the lead.

THE *Best* WORST NEWS

The best worst news is that he doesn't *want* you to call, so that should make it easier to harness the compulsion to do so. Cold turkey sucks, but it's the fastest route to recovery. That goes for every addiction known to man, from gambling to Cadbury Crème Eggs and everything in between—including obsessive calling, e-mailing, and IMing with your ex.

But why can't I call him? you ask. Why can't I just reach out and talk to him if it will make me feel a little better? After all, he does have that sweater of mine I never liked, and I really should call him to get it back. These are the questions that will be running through your mind, and the answer is—we'll say it again—because he doesn't want to talk to you. Even if you think that he does, you're probably wrong. If he wanted to talk to you, to check on you, to reconcile with you, he would. If he had the courage to break it off, he also has the ability to use the phone and dial your number, which is already committed to memory. All the broken fingers in the world won't keep someone who's truly determined from calling, so any excuse you can think of is just that, an excuse. And quite frankly, even if you don't want to hear it, the fact that he doesn't want to talk to you is actually a GOOD THING! It's just the kind of slap in the face that should make getting past this stage of the breakup easier.

Even more to the point is that NOT CALLING him eventually sends the bigger message. It speaks volumes and says, "Despite the heartache and loss, the reason you are not hearing from me is that I am too busy taking care of myself and moving on with my fabulous new life." Isn't that the image you want to project and—more important—the person who you want to be? A person who is not hung up in the past but is instead moving forward? (Even if at the moment you're really just lying in your bed all day listening to sad songs in your pajamas.)

During these times, remember that the phone is your enemy—especially if you've been drinking. Leave your cell phone at home when you go out on a bender, and make sure your drinking companions know that you are to be kept away from phones at all times. There's nothing worse than blowing all your hard work and successful self-preservation on a drunk-dialing impulse. What better way to show someone they should still be with you than by calling them at your worst? More important, notice how you feel after you talk to him—and then ask yourself if that's really what you want.

WHAT I DID WRONG BY GREG

She made it pretty easy for me not to indulge in unbecoming and pathetic behavior because she moved to another state to be with DUDE. So, as painful as that was, at least she had the courtesy to do it in another zip code. It meant I didn't run the risk of bumping into her at parties and acting out a scene from the popular play *How the F*#k Could You Do This to Me I'm*

Dying on the Inside. There was no house for me to drive by or workplace I could stalk. All I had to do was not call her. I was okay during the day. But as soon as darkness fell, my new bestest buddy Tequila and I would find ourselves at a bar, or a party, or just drunk wandering around my kitchen having a chat, but soon we would have information. Here's the thing about Tequila: It gives you information. Information you didn't have prior to drinking it. Information that needs to get to the person who just smashed your heart. It is information that CANNOT wait 'til morning no matter what the hour. Tequila also has transformative qualities. It can turn the everyday ordinary telephone into a giant mistake-making machine that screams out to you, "Use me!" The phone calls were always the same. I'd just be calling to "check in." At 2:30 in the morning. Then I'd ask how she was doing. "Good, good. New York's kinda cold, but good." And then it would all go to hell with some version of "Why don't you love me?" or "Do you think we'll ever get back together?" Or the old chestnut "What's wrong with me?" Basically, questions that had already been answered, that couldn't be answered, or were self-evident. To be fair to her, she was incredibly gracious to me as I rambled on like a drunken Morrissey song for sometimes up to two hours. I would have not been so gracious had the shoe been on the other foot. Even writing this now I want to hang up on me. I want to hang up on you. I want to hang up every phone everywhere. It makes my stomach hurt to think of how low I was and how I plagued this person for not being in love with me. And I am embarrassed that no matter how great I feel in my best moments, there is one person in the world who can say, "Well, this one time . . ."

How I Got Through It by Amiira

After about a year and a half of marriage, my first husband and I separated (his idea) but remained in couples therapy (my idea). It became relatively clear that we were moving more toward divorce than reconciliation, and I was crushed. So our therapist suggested that we try to go thirty days without any contact to see how the reality of not being in each other's lives felt. No talking on the phone or in person. Are you kidding me? Do I look like I'm made of wood? That's like asking me to climb Mount Everest in strappy Manolos. I'm not at all conditioned for this kind of workout. Aren't you supposed to ease me into the idea? Wean me off of him over the course of a few months? It sounded like an impossible task. Even though we had been separated, we were still talking every day, taking the subway to work together sometimes, and spending a good amount of time together. Dinners, rock shows, did I mention that we took the subway together? Clearly, I needed to remind our therapist that he was my best friend and that even if we didn't make it as a couple, we were pretty set on staying friends, so this whole "No Contact" thing didn't really apply to us. When I informed her of this, she stared at me blankly as though I had failed to make a valid point of any kind and suggested that we begin the thirty days in the morning.

Is she crazy? I thought. I can't go thirty days without talking to him. That day he and I talked on the phone until midnight and then said good-bye for a month. At 12:01, I felt like calling him right back to say that I couldn't do it, but instead I turned on the TV and made myself go to sleep. Surely I could last overnight while I was sleeping. The next morning was harder. But I made myself get through the day, and every time I wanted to call him I called my friend Janet instead. I can't tell you how often I thought about calling him in those thirty days, because for the first two weeks the number would have to be in the thousands. And you can imagine how many times I called Janet during those two weeks. It was like an endurance test. But I was determined to get through those thirty days. I realized that if this was the beginning of the end and I was about to spend the rest of my life not talking to him, then I had better get used to it.

So for the first two weeks I thought of pretty much nothing else. But then the most amazing thing happened. I realized that I had gotten through TWO WHOLE WEEKS! That's FOUR-TEEN WHOLE DAYS of not talking to him, and suddenly I became wildly impressed with myself. I was Superhuman. I spent more time congratulating myself on being so kick-ass than I did thinking about calling him. The reward of my own strength during an incredibly weak time and the pride I felt by getting through each day without caving in and calling him was unbelievably empowering. It was like my strength fed itself once I finally got over the hump. It was hard. I thought about calling every second of every day . . . until I didn't anymore. And you know what? On the twenty-seventh day, he called me. He didn't make it to thirty days. He said it was one of the hardest things he's ever had to do. And it was. But the feeling I got from being stronger than my weaknesses far outweighed its being hard by a mile. Feeling great about yourself makes you feel invincible, and that's how I felt. Which is a long way from where I was on day one. And while I hated that therapist for sentencing me to such a harsh reality, I would have never known what that felt like if I'd continued to be a slave to the phone.

AWESOME THOUGHT The phone can also be used to call your mom or anyone else who loves you . . . except babies and dogs. They can't answer the phone.

SAD PERSON'S

Journeywork Workbook and Sometimes Cookbook

Download the following ringtones from BroadwayBooks.com/gregbehrendtringtones and program them into your cell phone as your ex's personalized ring.

Ring Tone One: **REALLY:** Really? You're gonna answer it? Is that what we're doing now—backsliding? Really, we're just gonna chuck our self-esteem out the window?

Ring Tone Two: **VOICE MAIL:** Let it go to voice mail. Let it go to voice mail. You are too busy getting on with your life. Let it go to voice mail.

Ring Tone Three: **DELETE:** Seriously, why haven't you deleted this number? C'mon now, let's live in the future, Hot Stuff.

PSYCHO CONFESSIONAL

For a while he would take my calls and I would cry and scream and plead and beg, but after a couple of months he stopped taking them. It would always go to voice mail and he'd never call me back, probably because I said some pretty shitty things in those messages. I tried e-mailing him, but it was the same thing—he wouldn't respond, even when I put "I'm having your baby" in the subject line. I stalked him on his computer by instant messaging him until he changed his IM identity so that he no longer showed up on my buddy list. Finally, when I thought I had run out of ideas, I remembered he and I both had phone cams and could e-mail each other pictures, so I sent him a picture of me naked and now it's on the Internet. Next time I'd think about not contacting him.

Anonymous
Eugene, OR

TEN THINGS TO DO BESIDES CALL

1. Take yourself to a movie that he would NEVER have gone to with you.
2. Call an old friend that you've been meaning to catch up with.
3. Go window-shopping. (Just not for phones.)
4. Meet a friend for coffee.
5. Take your dog on a walk, OR go to the pound and rescue a pet on death row if you don't already have one.
6. Call your grandmother. You know it's been a while, and now's the perfect time to start lobbying for top placement in her will.
7. Put on one of your favorite CDs and dance around in your underwear. (Greg's idea.)
8. Go through your closet and get rid of everything that you wouldn't want to be seen wearing the next time you run into your ex.
9. Take a hike or a long walk and just enjoy being outdoors, or watch a fishing show on TV, which is kinda like being outdoors.
10. Go to the grocery store and get stuff to make your favorite meal for dinner.
11. Hey, Foxy, we already gave you ten ideas! Now come up with your own list.

Ten Things to Do Besides Call

1.

2.

3.

4.

5.

6.

7.

8.

9.

10.

INT. 7-ELEVEN—NIGHT

Bridgette, a twenty-two-year-old hipster in low-slung jeans, layered tank top, and flip-flops, stands at the cash register unloading her goods. She lays down a case of beer, two pints of Ben & Jerry's ice cream, a bag of Doritos, assorted candy bars, and tabloid magazines with headlines about celebrity breakups.

> CLERK

I'll need to see your ID.

Bridgette pulls it from her wallet and the clerk checks the D.O.B.

> BRIDGETTE

Can I also have two packs of Marlboro Lights and some matches?

The clerk reaches behind him and locates the cigarettes and matches and adds them to her pile. He scans the items.

> CLERK

Must be some party you're having.

> BRIDGETTE

Oh, no . . . this is just for me.

> CLERK

Ahhh . . . so how long were you guys going out?

                         BRIDGETTE

        Six months.

                          CLERK

        In that case, why don't you get the ice
        cream quarts instead of the pints, the
        Marlboro unfiltereds, and then go lay
        down in the parking lot and I'll back
        over you with my van.

                         BRIDGETTE

        What are you, my dad?

Bridgette glares at the clerk, puts back all of
her stuff, and returns to the counter with a copy
of *Runner's World* and two pints of water.

                         BRIDGETTE

        Smart-ass.

Chapter Three

HE'S NOT HIDING AT THE BOTTOM OF THAT PINT OF ICE CREAM

When you go through a breakup, we know it's natural to try to numb your pain by reaching out for things that make you feel good. Martinis. French fries. Coffee Heath Bar Crunch. That's why we chose an image of ice cream for our book cover—because it seemed to be the universal symbol of the comfort we all reach for when trying to get over a broken heart. Okay, so booze ran a close second, but we thought a picture of a half-empty Long Island Iced Tea and an ashtray of smoldering butts would be too depressing. It's completely natural to seek some kind of temporary relief and distraction from the pain you are experiencing right now. But while numbing yourself is a coping strategy, it's not an effective one. The feelings that accompany a traumatic breakup can easily lead to an avalanche of bad behavior. Harmless vices that you used to indulge in every once in a while—cigarettes, donut holes, blowing a week's salary on a pair of shoes—now suddenly become a way of life. But diving into a downward spiral doesn't hurt him—it only hurts you, and why would you want to do that?

Drowning your sorrows in the comforts of excess won't get him back—it'll only make you fatter, drunker, and sadder. Not that there's anything wrong with being fat, drunk, and sad—after all, look how it worked out for Ernest Hemingway. Breakups present an awesome opportunity for self-destructive behavior that often seems warranted but proves detrimental in the end. Whether you wake up in somebody else's bed, on the floor, or curled up inside an empty pizza box, this behavior only momentarily derails you from your agony. When you wake up, you'll be right back where you were the night before—still broken up, but now nursing a nasty hangover of excess or regret, and no further along on the road to recovery. Not that we're against a good romp in the hay, night on the town, or pint of Chunky Monkey—just understand that it's like putting a Band-Aid over a broken bone. It's not going to fix anything.

"Oh really?" you ask. "What should I do, then, stay home and read? Maybe I'll get my taxes done early or pop in a workout video." Let's not get carried away. We'd never ask you to do something as hateful as a workout video (unless you know of a really good one). We're merely suggesting that you lean into the idea of making healthier choices. Fun does not always have to come at the expense of your waistline or brain cells. You want to feel good about the choices you're making starting right now—not tomorrow morning, when you're hungover and making resolutions, or trying to broker a deal with God if he'll only take away your heartache.

Look, we applaud you for getting out of the house. In fact, getting out of the house is one of the best steps you can take. Go out with your friends. Put yourself in the driver's seat and start moving on with your life. Just try to be smart about it. Trying to soothe yourself during tough times is natural, and we encourage that. However, self-destructive behavior masked as soothing your-self is what we want to steer you away from. Look, we're no saints. We've made bad decisions along the torturous road of breakups (that's why we feel suitably equipped to write this book), but we've learned that the momentary lapse of pain that occurs when you've dulled your senses with Cosmopolitans or over-loaded them with kisses from that not-so-attractive stranger in the bar is just that . . . MOMENTARY. It's fleeting and ultimately keeps you stuck in the pain longer. Every morning after, the sting of the breakup will come flooding back in and drag you back into the pits of despair. Only now, coupled with your grief, you'll most likely have regret: regret over all those carbs and fat calories you consumed, regret over sleeping with your best friend's boyfriend, regret over the packs of cigarettes and vodka tonics that make climbing the stairs an impossible chore.

Drinking, eating, shopping, revenge, rebound sex, drugs, or whatever your poison may be will numb the pain—but that's all. People by nature are very afraid to feel pain. But often the thought of pain is actually worse than the pain itself. It's never as bad as you think it's going to be. And you can't get over the heartbreak until you let yourself feel it. Sorry, Charlie, but that's the fact. It's like any grieving process—if you bury the pain deep down it will stay with you indefinitely, but if you open yourself to it, experi-ence it, and deal with it head-on, you'll find it begins to move on after a while. Putting down that pint of ice cream may not FEEL like the right thing to do, but if you change your behavior first, your feelings will follow. A very smart doctor once told us that. The behavior sometimes has to come before the feelings, so instead of doing something falsely satisfying that you'll regret, why not try doing something that you'll hate now (like deep-conditioning your hair and going to bed early) but be proud of later.

But Greg, I've Got Questions

But what's wrong with a few cocktails?

Dear Greg

My friends have been really great during my breakup. They meet me for happy hour or take me out for dinner a few times a week to keep my spirits up. Granted, a lot of the spirit lifting involves many cocktails and bashing my ex-boyfriend for being a loser and blowing it with the best thing that's ever happened to him. Just having friends to get drunk with who can comfort you when you're sad and vulnerable makes a breakup so much more deal-able. Don't you think that's part of the healing?
Patsy

Dear Happy Hour,
Treating your boyfriend to repeated celebrity roasts is great. What better way to get past someone than to keep talking about him? Don't get me wrong—it can be healthy to acknowledge your anger and talk it out with your pals who may also share some of the same

sentiments. Everyone heals differently. But what I know is that whenever I wallowed in cocktails, sadness, and vulnerability, it never made me feel any better, just sadder and more pitiful and a little puffy. The point is to get through this—not drag it out, unless, of course, that is what you want. So while it may momentarily make you feel better to belittle him, ask yourself this: Are you really healing when you're carrying around such anger?

But what's wrong with a little rebound sex?

Dear Greg

The only way to get over a good man is with another man—that's why the term "rebound" exists in the dating vocabulary. I spent months agonizing over my ex. Calling him all the time, showing up at his house, all the stuff that you're not supposed to do. I was just sad and miserable all the time. So my girlfriends told me that I needed to meet someone else. I decided that his roommate was someone else. You should have seen my ex-boyfriend's face the first time he saw me slip out of his best friend's room wearing only a man's pajama top. His jaw hit the floor, and I could tell it drove him crazy. I felt a whole lot better. What do you think about that?
Lexi

Dear Crazy Lady,
Wow! There's a whole lot of healthy going on in that scenario. I think your man would be very proud. Why don't you sleep with his favorite

sporting franchise? That will really show him! First off, sleeping with someone else to make another person mad is just mean. Why are you dragging an innocent party into your bummer of a relationship? It's not fair or healthy. Second, I bet it only felt good in the moment and didn't take you any further away from the pain you were in and probably made things worse for all involved. Third, if you think that your ex thinks anything other than that you're a skanky you-know-what . . . then you've been eating paint. The best thing you can do is get out of your ex's world and go find someone real to love. Any relationship that's designed solely to elicit a reaction from someone else is not only false but a major discredit to anyone who's a part of it. When you truly move on, you won't care what your ex thinks. And for the record, the best revenge isn't messing up his life—it's getting on with yours and living it to the fullest.

> ## But eating is the only thing that makes me feel better.

Dear Greg

My fiancé broke up with me and now I can't stop eating. It's the only thing that makes me feel better. He's already dating another woman, and it's only been a month since he asked for the ring back. I've never been in such agony in my whole life. We still have to see each other because we had bought a house together, and he shows up with his new girlfriend every time we have to meet. It's so hurtful and humiliating that I end up sitting in my car crying with a bag of chips for an hour. I feel pathetic on top of heartbroken. Help!
Jenna

Dear Hungry Hearted,

Put down the chips and wipe your tears (and your fingers too). I totally get it. I love chips, especially the salt and vinegar ones! I know the momentary instantaneous pleasure they give can make you forget the pain you're in—at least for the short term—but the long-term effect on your self-esteem isn't worth it. Let's face it, there's nothing worse than feeling shitty about a failed relationship, and on top of that not being able to button your pants. I know that when I stroll around town with my pants held up by a rope, I don't feel great. Eating your way through a breakup won't make you feel better—just fatter and sadder, as you've noticed. The encounters with your ex and his new gal are serving as a trigger for every negative belief you hold about yourself. It's those insecurities, amplified by the pain of being faced with the woman he chose over you, that are sending you into this tailspin, and you've got to get control of it. So start by NOT seeing them. Send a friend, lawyer, realtor, or hired thug in your place to settle your business, and don't put yourself in that situation anymore. Next time, grab some celery and go for a walk. It's not tasty, but you will be if you take care of yourself.

But they're called painkillers for a reason.

Dear Greg

I had a bunch of Vicodin left over from when I had my wisdom teeth pulled. After a particularly bad night that included an embarrassing tearful call with my ex, I took one to make me feel better. And believe me, I felt better. So much so that I've worked my way through the bottle

and all of my friend's stashes as well. I know I shouldn't
be taking them, but it's the only thing that makes me feel
okay, or at least feel like I don't care. Do you think I have
a problem?
Courtney

Dear Vicodon't,
STOP THIS INSTANT! Yes, I do think you have a problem or are
quickly on the way to one. Is this the way you envision getting
through the rest of your days? Trust me as a recovering substance
abuser that you are not getting better—you are simply delaying
the process of working through the pain and creating an addic-
tion. The fact that you know you shouldn't be taking them and
are still doing so should be a major warning sign. Remember,
using substances to self-medicate is a temporary solution that
is destructive and only leads to more suffering. Seek profes-
sional help or get to a Narcotics or Alcoholics Anonymous
meeting ASAP. They are easy to find—just pick up the phone book.
No breakup is worth killing yourself over, and that's exactly
what you are on the road to doing. Please take it from someone
who knows.

How many flings is too many?

Dear Greg

Since my boyfriend and I broke up, the only time I don't
think about him is when I'm hooking up with someone
else. After the breakup, my roommates encouraged me
to "get back on the horse" and would take me barhopping

to meet new guys. Now they say that they're worried about me because I've got all these random guys calling and stopping by the house at all hours. I thought they were just being overly protective, but then I realized that I don't really remember some of the guys because of how drunk I was. All I was doing was trying to erase the memory of my ex, and now I'm starting to feel a little freaked out. It's the only thing that made me feel good, but now it's making me feel even lonelier and more depressed. What do I do?

Leanne

Dear Cowgirl,
Getting back on the dating horse and having sex with the whole corral are two very different things. I'm sure your friends didn't mean for you to go out and indulge in self-destructive behavior. It's one thing to go out to a bar and flirt, maybe even make out with someone new, just to know that you are still desirable, but you can't sleep your old boyfriend away. Certainly, meeting new people is a great idea, but try DATING! As in dinner and a movie peppered with conversation. You are going through a rough patch, and you are just going to have to ride it out. So start by getting rid of the random dudes—tell them you're not interested, change your phone number if you have to—and then work on allowing yourself to feel your feelings. They will subside in time. And remember, having sex is fine, but using sex to push away bad feelings is just super unhealthy, and that's not what you are all about, Cowgirl.

A Quick Note on Rebounding BY AMIIRA

When you're feeling down and lonely, there's nothing like a little positive attention from the opposite sex to snap you right out of the dumps. A little makeout session, some heavy petting, or even a roll in the hay. Sometimes a little affection is just what the doctor ordered and certainly one of the first things that the heartbroken will seek. The thing about rebounding is it can go both ways: It can make you feel great—or it can make you feel awful. You might meet someone really interesting and have a lovely affair that rebounds you right out of your heartbreak and back into the world. But that's not always the case.

When you're vulnerable and looking for some validation from a stranger, the opportunities for things to go south are plentiful. You can go out for the evening determined to find someone to hook up with, and end up feeling even more pathetic if no one will flirt with you. Or you can end up going home with someone whom you'd never pay attention to otherwise, then regret it the next day when you're shamefully trying to locate your clothes. You can have a one-night stand and think you are cool with it, but then, when the guy doesn't call like he promised to, feel rejected all over again. You can end up heaping pain on top of pain.

Navigating the rebound waters can be tricky, and I've been fortunate to make it through with relatively few regrets. I tended to rebound with old boyfriends rather than new acquaintances, because there is always a certain level of security you feel with an ex (although reopening those doors can get sticky too). But since rebounding can be a particularly risky coping strategy, with the potential to do even more damage to your romantic self-esteem, you should try to set some ground rules and standards. Mine were pretty simple yet clear:

1. Don't rebound with anyone who compromises your job or makes going to work uncomfortable.

2. Try to pick someone whom you would be drawn to under normal circumstances.

3. The cuter the better!

4. No need to hand out home runs when a base hit will satisfy your ego.

5. If you're too drunk to drive, you're too drunk to make good decisions. Abort the mission immediately.

6. Stay away from your ex's friends. Stay away from *your* friends and your best friend's ex-boyfriends.

7. Buy a vibrator. It'll never call when you don't want it to.

8. I don't care how cool or jaded you are—sex is still intimate even if there are handcuffs involved.

9. The person you are having sex with is also a person.

10. Before you look for validation in others, try and find it in yourself.

THE *Best* WORST NEWS

The best worst news is that you *know* when you are indulging in self-destructive behavior to numb you from the heartbreak that is rocking you. Much like you *know* when you're about to do something wrong, it's an awareness that is built into all of us humans (unlike flies, who will eat ice cream until they explode). There's an actual moment in which you consciously decide whether or not to take the plunge and act on the impulse. Knowing that this moment exists means that you have a choice, you have control—and hopefully one of these times you'll exercise that control and make the better choice when you're staring down the barrel of your fifth drink or before you climb into that stranger's bed.

Breakups can often feel like a crisis. And a person's character can be measured by how they act in a crisis. You can either fall apart or rise to the challenge of pulling yourself out of the shit storm. As two people who have experimented with both options, we must tell you, going down in flames, booze, food, one-night stands, and mind-altering substances is *No Bueno*, whereas being the hero in the production of "My Heart Has Been Blown to Pieces" is life-altering, life-affirming, and f*#king sweet! You have a choice. You get to drive. That's the good news. You actually have an opportunity to prove that you are a person who can handle an emotional disaster. Hey, just the fact that you didn't fly off the rails will not only impress your friends, but will also earn you some much-needed self-respect. So MapQuest your ass on the road to recovery—not Sadville, population Drunky the Clown, aka: YOU.

It's an odd thing to think about, but try imagining that your breakup is a disease. If you were told that you had a serious yet curable disease, would you go get hammered on a regular basis? Eat two bags of Oreos? Chain-smoke, pop pills, get stoned, or f*#k around? NO YOU WOULDN'T. You would take great care of yourself and cut all the unhealthy things out of your life. Because you love yourself, and even if you don't right now, WE DO! So put down the _____ and start moving on.

(insert vice here)

WHAT I DID WRONG BY GREG

August 12, 1996, 11:32 A.M. "I'm fat." I can't suck my gut in. From where my sweaty head rests on the pillow, I can see that my belly sticks out beyond my chest and rests on my single-guy futon. (I can already tell this is going to be a great day.) My brain is swimming in a wet headache and I can smell last night on my breath. I roll over to greet my bedmate. "Hello, stranger." But it's not a stranger; in fact, it's not a person at all. It's a traffic cone and a street sign that I must have made friends with on my journey home last night. Did I have sex with a traffic cone? No matter how much you try, a traffic cone cannot replace your ex. When did I become this guy? Who is this guy?

I don't know why the voice inside us that wants us to win and make the right and sometimes difficult decisions is so quiet, and the one that wants us to self-destruct can be so loud and persuasive. But on this particular morning, the quiet one demanded to be heard: "Hey, dummy! Why are you doing this to me? What did I do to get you to hate me so much? Why do you want to be so miserable?" "I don't," I answered back. "It's not me, it's her. It's her fault I'm like this." But the voice wasn't having it: "Bullshit. She's not the one pouring booze down your throat, you are! She's not the one in bed with a rebound cone. This is all you, buddy, you are the playwright of this drama." The voice was right. This was not what I was supposed to be. The world was going on without me. She had gone on without me.

On August 12, 1996, 12:30 P.M., I attended my first meeting of Alcoholics Anonymous, and since that day I have, one day at a time, remained drug and alcohol free. It was the first step on the long road back to myself. This time the quiet voice won.

How I Got Through It by Amiira

For years I was stuck in a wildly unhealthy pattern in my relationship. It went like this: Things are great, we're in love, we're inseparable, I feel happy all the time, we have so much fun, the sex is good but infrequent (something we're going to work on). THEN he starts acting weird, distant, and picks fights with me until he reveals that he doesn't think he wants to be in a relationship anymore. He drops the "I think we should take a break" bomb and we're not having sex anymore, I feel sad and rejected all the time, and he moves out and has sex with strippers. I do a lot of crying and feel even worse about myself because he'd rather have sex with strippers than with me, and it seems like we're headed for a real split rather than a break . . . THEN he comes back to me and wants us to get back together, he pledges his undying love, and promises he'll do whatever it takes to make it up to me. Things start off strong, he goes to therapy . . . THEN, after months of us being back together, things start feeling bad again; he stops wanting to have sex and is no longer making an effort to work on our problems or repair things between us. I confront him about it, and he admits that he's lost interest in the idea of working on it because it's too hard. He says he thinks we should take a break. Start vicious cycle over. Lather, rinse, and repeat.

This is what I endured for years. I say "endure" rather than "was subjected to" because if I had been a stronger woman at the time, I would have recognized the situation for what it was and just left with my dignity in hand. But I was in love with him, or maybe just in love with the idea of the way we'd been, and this kept me prisoner in a self-esteem-crushing purgatory. The point is that no one kept me there but me, though at the time it seemed like I was the victim of his problems and general f*#ked-up nature. Now, to be fair to myself, I was married to this person. I had made a commitment that I took seriously and planned on spending my life with him, so I put up with things that I wouldn't have ever imagined accepting because I was sticking it out for our future. Marriages have ups and downs, but mine had more downs than ups, and even though the ups were a lot of fun they were still riddled with intimacy issues that left me feeling bad about myself. On top of that, he was having sex with other women when we were on a break (which I always told myself didn't really qualify as cheating). Regardless, it still felt shitty. I was always the one who was heartbroken, and even so, couldn't imagine being with another man.

So after years of this, I FINALLY recognized that it was never going to get better and that I was wasting good years of my life in a dysfunctional relationship. I knew I had to get out, and yet I also knew that I was powerless with this man and that my desire for the relationship to work was crippling. These were all things I could see clearly by this point. So as we headed for another separation/break, I made a conscious decision that this time around I was going to force myself to behave in a way that was the complete opposite of the way I'd behaved before. Instead of spending my time feeling sorry for myself and drowning my sorrows in wine, I got my ass on the StairMaster every day and furiously climbed away to my favorite breakup record (*Everything's Different Now* by 'Til Tuesday). I went to my hairdresser and had him cut my long hair short and lighten it. I was determined to undergo a transformation, and I wanted to be reminded of it every time I looked in the mirror. It was my own little statement that I AM DIFFERENT NOW.

I also got out into the world instead of retreating from my social life and actually met a guy. He was a bit younger, but from our first conversation it was clear that we had a connection as well as immediate chemistry. We became good friends who did a lot of flirting. I worked hard at my job, kept myself busy, spent a lot of time with my friends, and gained confidence every time I caught a glimpse of my short-haired reflection and remembered that I AM DIFFERENT NOW. This time, when my husband made it clear that we were done (again), I was deeply saddened but thankful for his honesty and made the decision that I was finally going to move on with my life. And the next time I spoke with my new flirtation, I told him that my marriage was over, and he asked me out. Normally, I would have said something along the lines of "It's too soon and I'm not ready to even entertain the idea of dating," but instead I stayed firm to my rule of taking the opposite action and said, "YES!" We went out, and it was great. So we went out again, and it was even better. And we started seeing each other on a fairly regular basis, and after a while I had sex with him! Something I could have never done or even thought of only a few months prior—and you know what? It was the most liberating thing I have ever done for myself. I wasn't having sex to spite my estranged husband; I'd had sex because I wanted to and because I KNEW that if I did I would never go back to that unhealthy relationship that I'd been going back to again and again for years. I was crossing a line and I couldn't go back. But I had done it consciously, in my own time. I took an opposite action because I was different now, and it freed me.

★★Note from Greg. "Uh, what? You had sex with who?"

AWESOME THOUGHT Alone also means available for someone outstanding.

SAD PERSON'S

Journeywork Workbook and Sometimes Cookbook

Overindulgence, like great art, is in the eye of the beholder. In other words, how can you tell if you are really pushing the envelope on what's safe and what's not? Take our little test below to find out. Give yourself five points for every statement that rings true.

1. When someone yells, "Hey, Boozebag!" you automatically turn around.
2. The guy you buy your pot from considers you family.
3. You are dating both Ben and Jerry.
4. The shopping mall has named a wing after you.
5. Jack Daniel's has offered you a sponsorship.
6. You hear yourself say things like "I don't know, I think clowns are kind of sexy."
7. The guy you buy pot from wants to get married.
8. Domino's has you on their speed dial!
9. You've taken up smoking to kill the time between eating and drinking.
10. The guy you buy pot from thinks you should get your shit together.

If you scored even five points, you've got problems, pretty lady. This was obviously just for fun, but seriously—take care of yourself. No one is worth self-destructing over. No one.

PSYCHO CONFESSIONAL

'd never been much of a drinker, but when my college boyfriend dumped me for no apparent reason, I became quite acquainted with the apple martini. At first it really took the edge off, but I found out (mostly from friends) that the drunker I got the more reckless and daring I got. I thought everyone was just being overly dramatic until Halloween. I had dressed up as a harem girl and looked quite fetching, if I do say so myself. After a few martinis, I felt like my ex should get a gander at what he was missing, so I marched over to his house in the freezing cold. He didn't appear to be home, so I let myself in with the key I still had and decided to wait for him in his bed. Then, from what I can gather, this is what happened next: I must have heard him arrive home and panicked as he was coming up the stairs, and then scampered out onto his roof, forgetting that it was the dead of winter and the roof might be frozen. Well, I must have slipped, because I woke up the next morning in the bushes next to his front door. I'm soooo lucky I didn't break my freaking neck. His roommate found me there on his way to work and kindly drove me home. I'm drinking apple juice these days.

Anonymous
Sault Ste. Marie, MI

INT. OUTDOOR CAFE—DAY
Two women in their twenties, Portia and Dorrie,
are having coffee.

> DORRIE

I don't think I can see you anymore.

> PORTIA

Exactly! Except he said, "I don't *ever*
want to see you."

> DORRIE

No, *I* don't think I can see you.

> PORTIA

(annoyed) Uh . . . I was there, Dorrie, and he said, "I don't *ever* want
to see you."

> DORRIE

I know how he feels.

> PORTIA

You do? Because I have been racking my
brains trying to figure it out.

Dorrie gets up and rolls her eyes.

DORRIE

You're too much. This is all you ever
talk about. How can anyone be expected
to deal with you?

PORTIA

Is that what he told you? Did he say
I was too much?

Dorrie turns to leave.

DORRIE

I'm going now.

PORTIA

He said that too. That's so weird.
Except he said, "I'm going for good."
And I'm like, "You'll be back." Hey,
where are you going?

Chapter Four

IF YOU MENTION HIS NAME ONE MORE TIME ...

Your friends are going to break up with you too.

You may not have him, but you have something far more valuable right now—your friends. "Great. And my health, right? Oh, I'm so lucky." We know it sounds corny, but having good friends to call on will get you through the heartbreak you're feeling more quickly than you thought. Their love and companionship can be a beacon during your darkest hours—but believe us when we say that those beacons can go out. You want to take care of your friendships during this time, even as they are taking care of you. When you're on the other side, there's nothing worse than enduring the relentless chatter of the breakup-obsessed friend who doesn't listen to you or take your advice. Here's the thing to remember about your friends—they want you to be happy. They want you to be in a good, loving, and healthy relationship that inspires you to be the best you that you can be, not one that is difficult and painful. What's more, your friends can see your ex and your relationship for what it was—warts and all—and they probably aren't buying the rewritten version of the perfect love that you're pining over.

Six months from now, when you are in a completely different emotional space (if not already in a better relationship), you'll want to look back on this time and feel good about the way you behaved with the people around you. Not have visions of Lily Taylor singing "Joe Lies" and bumming out everyone at the party while her friends exchange uncomfortable glances. (If you haven't seen Cameron Crowe's film *Say Anything*, run, don't walk, to the video store. But don't wait for your ex to show up on your lawn with a boom box—it's just a movie.)

We know . . . your friends are always supposed to be there, but for the love of God, give them a break and stop talking about your ex for one minute! We all have those tapes that play in our head—what are they called? Oh yeah, thoughts. But some of them are meant just for you. You don't have to share every single one of them. In fact, stop listening to yourself! If you pay attention to your negative thoughts, you're only affirming their validity. Those thoughts are like a bratty child—if you pay attention to the bad behavior, it only encourages a bigger tantrum. We say this with the greatest measure of love and empathy, but take a step back and try to understand why you need to make a conscious effort not to subject your friends to endless questions, endless tears, and endless analysis during this time. It's one thing to get dumped by a guy, but it's another to get dumped by your friends, because they won't even have breakup sex with you.

You're great and your friends all know it. They're on call, ready and willing to help you get over that loser who wasn't right for you. However, right now you are stuck in the Melancholy Vortex of your breakup. It's an über-powerful trap that sucks you in and blinds you to all the bad, unhealthy, crappola times that were so glaring in your relationship, and it only plays back loops of the best moments, thus obliterating your sense of why it didn't work out. It's like *A Clockwork Orange*. You're figuratively stuck in that chair with your eyes held open by those weird eyelash-curler contraptions while movies of the two of you in your happiest times flash through your brain to classical music or Coldplay. Your friends, on the other hand, are saying, "Hey there, Hot, Smart, Happening Lady, why don't you stop strapping yourself into that chair and come sit with us?" And the reality is that if you don't start actually listening to them and taking their advice, your friends *will* tire of you. Open your mind to what they have to say, and whatever you do, DON'T blame them for pointing out your ex's less-than-admirable qualities, or trying to give you a reality check about your less-than-perfect relationship. That's what they're there for—to help you get up out of that chair and start moving on. In return, you need to set a time limit on how long you're going to dwell on the past. Try setting the limit at eight weeks. (When you get to Part Two of this book, we will tell you how you can and will achieve this.) If after eight weeks you still need to talk about it constantly, seek professional help and let your friends off the hook. Or talk to your dog. All the dog hears is "blah, blah, blah . . . ," which—take it from us—is what you are starting to sound like to your friends.

But Greg, I've Got Questions

But what if my friends are wrong?

Dear Greg

My boyfriend and I broke up three months ago after being together for almost four years. Even though it was a mutual decision, I'm wondering if it was the right one. My friends all think I need to get on with my life because I've spent my whole adult life with him (I'm three years out of college, which is where we met). They say I've been living in a vacuum and they're sick of hearing about it and never really liked him that much anyway. But the more I dissect it with them, the more I think they're wrong and just tired of hearing about it. What do you think?

Tamara

Dear Tamara Never Comes,

Here's the thing people forget: You are also in a relationship with your friends. These relationships will ultimately prove to be more profound than the one you just came out of, and right now, they are certainly more important. Your friends want what's best for you, and you need to recognize that they've been living through your relationship for as long as you have, because friends care about and share in each other's lives. So accept their opinions and move on. Not only should you trust your own instincts that getting out of the relationship was the right move, but the fact that your friends are backing your decision should only make you feel better about it. You should also trust your instinct when it tells you your friends are sick of hearing about your breakup. Give it a rest and take advantage of the other great things that good friends have to offer: fun, laughter, clothes to borrow, and best of all, activities that have nothing to do with your ex.

But isn't that what friends are for?

Dear Greg

It's been seven months since my boyfriend broke up with me. I feel like I'm in a really good place about it, considering that we'd been together for almost a year and were talking about marriage when out of nowhere he suddenly decided he didn't want to be in a relationship. But the main reason that I'm in a good place is because my friends let me talk about it all the time. It's my own process that I need to go through—exploring every possible explanation for why he had a change of heart and why I'm better off. And it helps to have an outlet for all the painful questions and emotions. My friends are the best, and I would absolutely do the same for them if the shoe was on the other foot. Seven months isn't that long to be still working it out, is it?

Janet

Dear Janet From a Sad Planet,
Seven months isn't too long if you're doing a Broadway play. But other than that—eesh! You are done! He's not in your life right now, so why is he still getting so much of your time and attention? Today is the day you stop tormenting yourself and your friends

over this. I've checked the limits on your friendship meters and they are at full. Give those good people a rest and move on before they do. You guys are never going to figure out why he broke your heart, and even if you do figure it out, the "why" will probably only serve to hurt you more without changing the reality of it. So accept that the relationship is over and get on with your kick-ass life. Talking about it is not acceptance—it's just resisting what is.

What if my best friend is still friends with him?

Dear Greg

I met my ex through my lifelong best friend Lindsey. She still sees him and hears about him all the time since they work for the same company, so naturally I feel like she should tell me what he's up to. How's he dealing with the breakup? Is he seeing anyone? Is he missing me but too afraid to tell me because I got so mad at him when we split? Recently, she told me she was tired of me grilling her for details and we had a massive fight. Am I wrong to think she should be keeping an eye on him for me? Isn't that what friends are for?
Coco

Dear Coco Loco,
Yes, you are wrong to demand answers from your friend. She's your ex's coworker, not a spy. She's told you she's uncomfortable with it and that's something you need to respect—otherwise, you are

not being a good friend to her. It's tough knowing that she has access to information about your ex that you don't, but the relationship you need to be most concerned about right now is the one between the two of you. Look at it this way: She's actually being really cool by not exposing you to information that is at best useless and at worst potentially hurtful. So what if he's going out with someone else? That's what happens when people break up. Knowing the details won't bring him back—rather, it keeps you caught up in the life of someone who's already moving on. It's called a breakup because it's broken—that's all the information you need.

Shouldn't my friends take sides?

Dear Greg

It's the worst. My ex and I have a lot of friends in common, so when he cheated on me I figured that most of them would take my side. But they haven't. In fact, it's as if nothing has happened at all. If they really are my friends, why won't they shun him? I know I can't ask them to do that, but I'm really hurt that they didn't do it on their own. How can they not be disgusted with him, and how can they not be mad at him for doing something so terrible to me? How do I handle this?
Robyn

Dear Friend in Need,
That sucks . . . it really does. It's hard to comprehend that a betrayal like cheating could be overlooked by people who sup-

posedly care for you. It sounds like your friends aren't sure how to deal with being in the middle of your breakup. Understand that you can't ask them to choose, but it's certainly worth having a conversation to let them know how you're feeling and to give them an opportunity to defend their allegiances. However, it's also clearly a time to pursue new friendships outside the circle that involves your ex-boyfriend, especially if you feel your current friends don't share your values. Divvying up the friends never goes smoothly when a couple breaks up; this same thing happened to me, and it hurt like hell when my friends didn't takes sides and wanted to remain friends with both of us. But ultimately it forced me to seek out new friendships—which actually led to meeting my wife. For more on this, see the box on page 101.

BONUS QUESTIONS

What if my friend is driving me crazy?

I want to break up with my best friend. I used to love her like a sister, but now I want to strangle her. You see, she was dating this guy we all hated named Mickey—he was a cheater, a drunk, and an all-around bad guy, and we were always pushing her to break up with him. Last spring she finally did it, and we were sooooo psyched, but now she won't stop talking about him and their completely dys-functional relationship. I didn't mind for the first few months, but it's been almost a year, and now I almost wish she'd get back together with him just so she'd shut up. Help!
Melissa

Dear Boston Strangler,

She only lost her guy a YEAR ago—give her a break! Kidding. Don't break up with your sad pal, just set some boundaries. As a friend, you have a duty to listen, but you also have a duty to let Sad Sally know she's testing the limits of the friendship. At this point, you are not doing her any favors by indulging her. By letting her know—in the nicest way possible—that you are done hearing about it, you are also letting her know that she has a problem, and maybe it will motivate her to speak to a professional or simply stop blathering on about Mickey the Rat. God, I hate that guy! If she can't handle your honesty and respect your boundaries, then you should consider benching this friendship for a while. You can always revisit and rekindle it later on when your friend is in a better place and has something else to talk about.

What if her "ex" is my dad?

Dear Greg

My dad left my mom after nearly twenty years of marriage because he "fell out of love" with her. I get that it sucks and hurts, and that my mom is in a lot of pain, but she won't stop talking about it. I'm almost sixteen and just starting to date myself, and she's really freaking me out. Every day it's another cautionary tale of ". . . and never let a man . . . because they all lie like your father." I feel awful for her. She cries all the time. She's angry. She's a mess. I live with her, so I know it's really ripping her apart, but he's MY DAD and I still love him. What can I do to be there for my mom but not take sides?

Trista

Dear Heartbreak Kid,
You've got to tell your mom to stop today! The thing is, you may be her friend, but you are definitely first and foremost her daughter, and she has an obligation to take care of *you*. Bagging on your dad is not healthy for either of you. You need to make her aware of what she's doing. Tell her how it makes you feel when she talks badly about your dad (example: "It really hurts me when you talk about Dad that way—I love him"). I'm sure she's not doing it on purpose, so tell her she needs to talk to a professional about it, or at the very least a friend that is not you. As for your dating life, let the experiences be your own, not your mom's. Remember, you can be supportive of your mom by doing nice things for her other than being her sounding board. Try to encourage her to seek more positive outlets for her energy. Good luck, Tiger!

THE *Best* WORST NEWS

We don't know what you've done in the past with other breakups, and maybe you don't remember either, but we'll bet your friends do. This means that if you haven't handled your previous breakups well, they're already bracing themselves for the torrent of tears, late-night phone calls, and one-note agonizing and obsessing that will make you not much fun to be around for the next few months. The good news is that you have an opportunity right now to decide to handle this breakup differently, unselfishly, and with poise. Resolve that you will be considerate of your friends and use them wisely. Yes, you've just broken up and it sucks, but there are ways to be responsible with your pain.

Divvying Up the Friends

There are few things harder on a friendship than when two mutual friends split up. And if we've learned anything from all of our breakups, it's that you'll always be surprised by the way the chips fall and the way friends take sides. It's like picking teams for a game of Red Rover, except that in this case the team captains don't get to pick; the players get to decide what team they want to be on—or if they even want to play at all. Having to take sides is almost impossible unless a clear line already exists or has been drawn by some really repugnant behavior. Usually what happens in a breakup is between the couple and nobody else. So with that in mind, when faced with this situation, we suggest that you take an honest look at the people you call your friends and what those friendships are based upon. The answers will help you get through the complexities and disappointments that can come during this time.

The friendships at stake basically boil down to three categories: your friends, his friends, and mutual friends.

Mutual Friends

The longer the relationship, the more mutual friends you are likely to have, and clearly these are the friendships that will be hardest to divide. Here's the thing: You don't have control of other

(continued on next page)

people—they are going to feel the way they feel and do what they're going to do. In the wake of their decisions, all you can do is decide what works for you, what *you* are comfortable with, and let the pieces fall where they may. Breakups can be hard on your friends too. They don't know what their allegiances should be, they'd rather not choose between you, and they probably wish you guys had just stayed together because it would have been so much simpler all around.

So make their lives easier and DON'T MAKE THEM PICK! Let them decide if they want to be your friend, his friend, or still friends with the both of you. Some friends won't want to get dragged into your breakup, and you'll have to respect that and decide if you can deal with that. For those friends who want to remain truly mutual, you'll need to set boundaries that work for both of you. Example: How comfortable are you with me talking about this? Will it bother you if I talk shit about my ex? Will it bother you if I don't want to be at the same parties or gatherings as him, and will you be okay doing things "just us" for a while? Then, if you find that it's just too hard to be around them because they are still friends with the guy who cheated on you, cut them from the team—or at least bench the friendship for a while.

His Friends

We know you loved his friends. They were so funny and cool, even his really sweet sister who became one of your best buds. But they are *his* friends. Don't pursue those friendships. If they want to be friends with you, they will make it known. Respect the fact that even though they like you, they probably don't want to hear about what a jerk he is and they'd rather you didn't ask for information about him. And be honest about why you want to be friends with them in the first place—hopefully, it's for their own winning qualities and not their proximity to him. Your friends are your friends. His are his—think of them like jeans: Just because you really love his jeans doesn't make them yours.

Your Friends

As we discussed earlier, your friends are one of the most valuable commodities you may have right now. While some of them may have become friends with your ex, unless you've really become a complete nightmare, they are probably all going to fall into your camp with no questions asked. There may be one or two who remain acquaintances with your ex if the breakup was amicable or if special circumstances exist (like they work in the same field). You have to decide if you're cool with that and have an honest conversation about it. Your real friends should respect your needs during this time and do what they can to support you. In return, you can make them brownies (see page 107) or at least make sure that they feel loved and appreciated for their importance in your life.

One suggestion: Call your best friends and tell them, "Hey, I'm in the dumps right now and I'm going to need your help." Let them know this might take some time but if you could have at least an hour of time a day from one of them you'd be grateful. This way you can exercise the need to be sad and rambling on without forcing one or two of them to bear the brunt and wearing out your welcome. They will surely oblige you (unless your friends suck). Not only that, but since you have been kind enough to ask, they will probably take great pains to get through this with you. Just let them know you care about them too. Most important, listen to their opinions and what they have to say—they are your friends because they love you. Their encouragement and insight will guide you through this heartache, but you have to take those tear-soaked tissues out of your ears to actually *hear* them. Why did you put them in your ears, anyway?

WHAT I DID WRONG BY GREG

Greg! If you don't stop, I gonna punch you in the neck." But you don't know what I'm going through, man. "Yes, sadly I do, because it's all you've talked about for the last six months." I know, but it helps to talk about it. "I would have to disagree with that statement. You seem to be just as bummed now as you were when it first happened, except now *I* don't like you." But you are my friend. "Yes, but you don't listen to me. I've made suggestions about how you can get through this, I've tried to get you involved in other types of activity besides drinking and feeling sorry for yourself, and I've even recommended that you get professional help. But I've realized you're not talking to me, you're talking *at* me. You don't want help. You want to feel like shit. You like having something to be miserable about, so I'm gonna let you do it alone, because quite honestly I can't f*#k-ing take any more Boo Hoo Jones." Wow, harsh! But that's essentially the conversation I had with more than a few of my good friends and a couple of bartenders as well. The thing is, it took a while to repair those friendships, so for a while not only was I without a woman to love, I was also out of friends. Friends are all we have sometimes, and it's in these dark days that we need to not only appreciate them but also listen to them and really make an effort to consider what they are saying. Whether you know it or not, they went through the relationship with you and may have some insight and perspective. So for God's sake stop talking about your EX!

How I Got Through It by Amiira

As I mentioned earlier, I really leaned on my friends from the first second of my big breakup. I drafted them into duty, and they showed up in uniform mere moments later to help propel me through my agony. They were certainly sympathetic *to a point,* but they had accepted long before I did that my relationship stunk. They had put up with my misery and excuses while I was in said stinky relationship, so when it ended it was no surprise to my inner circle, just a collective sigh of relief. We often don't realize it, but our friends also live through our relationships as secondhand observers, so they can be objective about things that we can't. This is a blessing. Every time I would get sad or melancholy about something that was great about my ex, my friends would pummel me with twenty things that weren't great. They didn't allow me to slip on the rose-colored glasses and romanticize the past. They made me see my relationship for what it was now and what it had really been like all these years. They appealed to my logic, my pride, my hopes and dreams of what love was supposed to be like, and it made me see clearly that even if my heart hurt and I wanted to be back in that shitty relationship because the world unfolding before me was new and strange, I, as a self-aware person with a modicum of self-respect, SHOULDN'T BE.

AWESOME THOUGHT Even Halle Berry has been dumped. (What dummy made that decision?)

Journeywork Workbook and Sometimes Cookbook

Write down every thought you're having about your ex on a piece of paper. Every unanswered question, regret, malicious thought, sexy detail, melancholy rambling, song lyric, thing that drove you crazy, glaring flaw, secret thing that only you know, and so on . . . Now crumple that paper into a ball, throw it into the trash, and take a mental picture of it there. That's what the inside of your best friend's head looks like when you keep talking about it.

Maybe it's time to show your friends how much you appreciate them by making them some of Amiira's Famous Crack Brownies (no illegal substances involved). We promise that all will be forgiven upon the first bite!

Crack Brownies

> 50 light caramels
>
> ⅓ cup skim evaporated milk
>
> 1 package German chocolate cake mix
>
> ¾ cup melted butter (not margarine)
>
> ⅓ cup skim evaporated milk (yes, another ⅓ cup)
>
> 2 cups milk chocolate chips (or semisweet if you're that kind of gal)

Preheat oven to 350°F/180°C. In heavy saucepan, combine caramels and ⅓ cup evaporated milk. Cook over low heat, stirring constantly, until caramels are melted. Grease and flour a 9" × 13" baking dish. In a large mixing bowl, combine dry cake mix, melted butter, and the other ⅓ cup evaporated milk. Stir by hand until the dough holds together. Divide dough in half and press first half of dough into prepared baking dish. Bake at 350°F/180°C for 8 to 9 minutes. Remove from oven and sprinkle chocolate chips over baked crust. Pour caramel mixture over the chocolate chips. Crumble the other half of the dough over caramel layer. Return to oven and bake for 20 minutes. Remove and cool for 15 minutes, then cut into squares. Refrigerate for at least 30 minutes before serving. Return to refrigerator when not eating, as they get goopy at room temperature.

Now invite your friends over for dessert and make a pact with yourself to talk about *them,* not *you,* the entire time!

PSYCHO CONFESSIONAL

When my boyfriend broke up with me, I literally lost my mind. I couldn't stop obsessing about him and drove my friends away one by one. At first they started screening their calls, then many of them stopped returning my calls. I finally got the hint when three of my friends got new cell phone numbers and couldn't remember what their new numbers were whenever I asked for them. Finally, I sat down my oldest friend and demanded to know what was going on. Aren't friends supposed to help you through this time? Well, with as much love as she could muster, she told me that I'd gone over the edge when I burned my name into my ex's front lawn with fertilizer. As sympathetic as they wanted to be, vandalism was where they drew the line. After that, I started seeing a therapist, and one by one my friends have let me have their numbers again.

Anonymous
Lawrence, KS

INT. BEDROOM—DAY
The curtains are drawn and the bed and floor are littered with evidence that someone has been camped out here for a while (movie boxes, take-out food containers, etc.).

From under the covers we hear . . .

SHANA

I'm still not feeling very well. I think I'm going to stay home today. (Pause) What? (Pause) But I've only been out for a few weeks. . . . (Pause) What do you mean I don't work there anymore? (Pause) When did I get fired? (Pause) Oh . . . Do I have to get out of bed to file for unemployment?

Chapter Five

STOP CALLING IN SICK

hat time is it when you've hit the snooze alarm fifty-two times? Time to realize you can't sleep through a breakup. Although it does feel good, we'll grant you that. Escaping into the murky darkness of sleep provides some relief—however, it's an escape from reality that keeps you from dealing with what's really going on. "But I'm so cozy here in bed," you plead. Indeed, but soon that will wear off, especially after you get fired from your job and your power is shut off because you were too sleepy to write a check to the electric company and go to the mailbox.

On the other hand, there are those of us who lie in bed awake night after night praying that the Sandman will grant them a moment's sleep, a reprieve from their misery. These are the poor souls whose anxiety-riddled minds give them no rest as they replay the endless tape of "Why? Why? Why?" Whichever category you fall under, our advice to you is the same. Don't call in sick again today. You can't avoid your life.

Look, he already took your heart and spirit—now you're going to give him your job too? In times like these, you should be totally psyched to have a place to go every day. A place that's all about you and what you can accomplish, regardless of your relationship status. Embrace your boss (not literally, because that would confuse things) and ask him to pile it on. Idle hands are the Devil's text messagers. Work is the best thing you could have right now. It takes you outside yourself, because you are accountable to someone or something else besides your couch and that *Sex and the City* marathon. If you don't have a job, maybe it's time to get one. And it's not going to happen in bed. Not many bosses think, "I'm looking for an employee who sleeps a lot."

When either complete lethargy or sleeplessness is afflicting you, you may be suffering from depression. We're not saying that those symptoms aren't real or that they are unwarranted. But know that they can be like quicksand. Once you get sucked into this kind of pattern, it's hard to get out. Not having the energy to do anything other than feel sorry for yourself is in itself a symptom of depression. And like any other problem, you have to be able to recognize it before you can do anything about it.

This is why we say, Dive into your job! Run headfirst into your life. Fight back that urge to curl up in the fetal position, and fill your days with as much activity as you can tolerate. Call that old friend that you've been meaning to talk to, download all your CDs to your iPod, or dust off that piano in the corner. Keeping yourself busy, and your mind occupied, will get you through these times and prevent true depression from setting in. We know it sucks, but you need to force yourself out of that comfy, cozy cocoon of a bed and get back to your rocking butterfly self.

But Greg, I've Got Questions

But what if I can't get out of bed?

Dear Greg

After my boyfriend broke up with me, I didn't get out of bed for a month. I couldn't eat, find a reason to shower, or even get out of my pajamas, much less drag my ass out of the house. All I could do was sleep. I didn't even open the curtains in my room. I was in mourning. I skipped all my classes and ended up taking incompletes in some of my courses, so now I have to finish my classes over the summer. I'm not really ready to deal with my life again, but I don't want to drop out of college over this guy. How do I get back on the horse, as they say, when I barely have the strength to get out of bed?

Callie

Dear Going Back to Callie,
You just do it! You tell yourself, "I mourned this guy for a semester, and now he is done ruining me and my life plans." Start simple. Get up and take a walk around the block. Call a friend to come walk with you so you will feel somewhat obligated. Once you've done that, set simple goals and work on achieving a few of them every day, like going to the store, calling your parents and friends, getting some cool new clothes for summer semester, and generally inching your way back to living like a normal Superfox. Believe me when I tell you he's not the only guy you'll ever love. In fact, you will probably know greater love—but you won't find him asleep

in your darkened room. (If you do meet a man in your darkened bedroom, consider it a red flag!)

But what if I don't know who I am anymore?

Dear Greg

I just went through the worst breakup imaginable. Three years of complete happiness just flushed down the drain because he couldn't keep his snake in his pants. I've never been so hurt and humiliated in my whole life. I even know the girl, because, if you can get this, she's his secretary. How f**king cliché. At first I sank so low that I didn't even have the energy to bathe. I just couldn't believe that my whole life had fallen apart. After a week and a half, I took a long look at myself and decided that the woman in the mirror with the greasy hair and stained T-shirt was not who I wanted to be. But I don't know who I am anymore, because my whole life revolved around him and the future we had planned together. What's next?
Emily

Dear Emily Post Breakup,
It's time to meet the new Emily. Who is she? I don't know, but she'll be stepping out of the shower any moment now, and when she does she's gonna put on her favorite jeans, her cutest top, do her hair and makeup (optional; not all ladies wear makeup— however, a little lip gloss does add luster), and take a long and loving look in the mirror and know that she is her own best comfort and friend. Today is the day you reclaim yourself and realize

that no matter who you are with, your life should never revolve around someone else's, Hot Stuff. He was not the Sun, he was more like Pluto or an asteroid or a gaseous cloud. The one thing people don't ever seem to get enough of is time for themselves. Well, now you've got it, and you can do anything you want with it. Even stuff you've never done, like race-car driving, surfing, or starting a band. Okay, so those are things I'd like to do, but you get the picture. He cheated on you once, but don't let him cheat you out of having a kick-ass life. Who is the new Emily? This is the time to start experimenting, start having fun, and find out.

But why am I taking it so hard?

Dear Greg

I can't sleep. I don't know if it's because I'm so used to sleeping with my ex-boyfriend that the bed feels too big, or if it's because I can't stop replaying "The Conversation" in my head and trying to look for clues where we went wrong. Either way, I'm going crazy, I look like hell, and my work is suffering. I've been late to meetings, late on reports, late to work, or sometimes not even shown up! I've been broken up with before and had even thought of breaking up with my ex a few times, but he beat me to the punch. What is happening to me?
Alix

Dear Alixer,
The brain really is an amazing thing—it has all kinds of ways to let you know you are in trouble. And the fact that you recognize that

certain aspects of your life are slipping means your brain wants to fix this but doesn't know how. If it's not getting any better, there are trained therapists, doctors, and psychiatric specialists who can be found in your phone book, online, or even through a friend. Sometimes we just can't think our way out of the way we are feeling, and there is no better way to solve the problem than reaching out to those who have made it their life's profession to help people do just that.

But what if I can't avoid him otherwise?

Dear Greg

My boyfriend and I broke up because I wanted to get married and he didn't. I know it's the right thing to do, because I really do want to get married someday and shouldn't waste my time with someone that "isn't the marrying kind." But we work together, so it's really awkward and painful every time we see each other, because I still love him. I've used up all my sick days and have been hibernating at home. I just can't face it. Do you think I'm being silly or weak if I ask to be transferred to another division so I don't have to see him anymore?
Genevieve

Dear Smartypants,
I think it's great that you are able to recognize that for your own self-preservation, a transfer is best. It's not weak at all—it's incredibly insightful. And it's not silly. Silly would be dressing up in a clown outfit and going to work hoping he wouldn't recognize

you. You're able to recognize that the relationship is broken and you're ready to move on—that rocks! I say you should not only go for the transfer but also cash in your vacation time the week before you move offices and take yourself somewhere nice. I wish more people had the courage to realize that the key to getting over someone is time away and putting yourself in a situation where you can win. Even if you don't get that transfer, there are also other jobs. Maybe this is a kickoff to a new career, because you are obviously smart, insightful, and employable. Get out of bed and do your best to be strong just a little longer—and put a smile on your face, because you're taking the steps you need to start a new chapter in your life.

THE *Best* WORST NEWS

The best worst news is that you've got your life back. I know what you're thinking: "I don't want my life back. I want my shitty relationship back." But your shitty relationship doesn't want *you* back. That doesn't mean there is anything wrong with you. Hell, he may actually be looking for someone worse because deep down he feels he is not worthy of you. Regardless, the person you were with has decided that you weren't the one for him. Or you decided it. Or you both decided it. Either way, it's a done deal. The shoe doesn't fit no matter how hard you jam your toes in there, so throw it away.

This time is a gift, and you should recognize that you might never have this opportunity again. The next relationship you get into might be the one that lasts forever, which is a great thought, but that also means you'll rarely have time alone again. So seize this opportunity to reinvent and better yourself. You have a chance to completely focus on you, which is a luxury that many of us don't get. Advance your career or decide on one, further your education, travel the world, build that bowling alley you've always wanted, get in great shape, read the books you haven't had time for, invent a new ice-cream flavor, or redecorate your living space and surround yourself in an inspiring setting. Embrace this time and spend it selfishly! Get on the road to becoming the person you dream of becoming, not the shell of the one sleeping her life away.

WHAT I DID WRONG BY GREG

It's easy to blow off a job you don't have. It's easy to not call friends you don't have, blow off a workout you don't have or a hobby you don't have. It's easy to defer a dream you don't have. But it's hard not having a life. When the smoke began to clear and I sobered up, I realized that the focus of my life had been her and the lack of her. You have to know this about me. I love being in love. I love butterflies and the rush of a first kiss. I love notes and e-mails and phone messages. I love the smells, the sounds, and the tastes. But at a different point in my life, I also loved being sad and f*#ked up, drinking excessively, listening to depressing indie rock, and sleeping through the day. I was either The Guy Who's in Love or The Guy Who's Been Crushed by Love. Both of these images gave me an identity. But when the dust from my über-breakup began to settle, I was suddenly The

Guy Without Any Plans, and that had to change. This is when I had the most amazing thought: "I get to start over." I know it doesn't sound amazing, let alone revolutionary, but that is exactly what it was. It's weird how you can hear certain words throughout your life and they bounce right off you. But when the reality of that situation hits you, when all you want is another chance, when you hate how you've been living and suddenly an option appears, those very words can be a life preserver. And in the blink of an eye, the world seemed full of possibilities. How it happened I don't know. But ever since I'd begun taking care of myself by getting out of bed, showering regularly, and leaving the house, I became increasingly open to new ideas because I began to truly feel and recognize that the way I'd been living wasn't doing it for me. Gosh, it only took me eight months to figure out that the first step was getting out of bed every day.

How I Got Through It by Amiira

J was one of the sleepless. I felt sick to my stomach all the time and I couldn't even think of eating. My sorrow manifested itself in a truly physical way, and my stomach became an empty pit of sadness. I felt so physically ill every time my relationship took a downward turn that I would have been completely debilitated if I hadn't had such a strong will and a high threshold for pain (two traits that I'm grateful for). Each time my ex-husband drove our relationship into the murky waters of "I don't know if I'm in love with you" or down the river of "I don't want to be married," my weight would plummet and the dark circles would settle in under my eyes. I looked like hell, a sad and sickly girl walking through the world.

But you know what I did have? A great job, a very cool boss, awesome friends, and a StairMaster 4000PT. I really loved my job as a record executive, and I was beyond grateful to have meetings to attend, deadlines to meet, marketing plans to create, and bands to see. I would go in early, because I certainly wasn't sleeping. I dedicated myself to working my ass off, and I felt relief and satisfaction from doing my job well in spite of my situation. I filled my downtime by reading books, listening to music, talking with friends, watching movies, working out, and doing anything besides allowing myself to get caught in the vortex of overthinking. And you know what? All of that activity balanced out my misery. My focus was on nurturing the other parts of my life so that I didn't feel so empty, lost, and sick about the demise of my marriage. I wasn't letting a relationship and person that I had absolutely no control over defeat me anymore. In all other aspects of my life I was happening—which gave me not only a sense of self but also something to hold on to and a foundation to rebuild from.

AWESOME THOUGHT Having someplace to go, like a job, is a good thing. That's eight hours a day when you have to think about something else besides your relationship (at least a little bit).

Journeywork Workbook and Sometimes Cookbook

SAD LIBS (The Sad Person's Mad-Libs)

Bedsores and Boo Hoos

Once upon a time there was this _____ gal named
                                    (super positive adjective)

_____. Her _____ness was unquestionable. All the _____
(your name)   (adjective)   (plural noun)

around knew that she was the cat's _____. One such ____
                                   (sleepwear)   (noun)

worked especially hard to get her attention. He was so _____
                                                       (adjective)

and _____ that _____ couldn't resist. Many thought
    (weather condition)   (your name)

she was _____ for going out with _____ in the
        (negative adjective)   (your ex's name)

first place. After _____ long months of _____ times, things
                   (insert number)   (adjective)

started to get really _____. Then out of nowhere things _____
                      (adjective)   (adverb)

came to an end. Everyone thought that _____ was a com-
                                       (your ex's name)

plete _____ and should go _____ himself. But even that didn't
      (noun)   (verb)

make _____ feel better, so she retreated to her _____ and was
     (your name)   (noun)

overcome with _____. After_____ her wounds, she picked
              (noun)   (-ing verb)

herself up and decided that today was the _____ day to reclaim
                                          (adjective)

her life. "_____ him," she shouted as she _____ out of
          (Expletive)   (verb, past tense)

bed and _____ to the shower. She deep-conditioned her
         (verb, past tense)

_____ and shaved her _____. Wiping the fog from the bath-
(noun)   (plural noun)

room mirror, she _____ at her reflection and said aloud,
                 (verb, past tense)

"Hello, Hot Stuff!" From that day forward, _____ never
                                             (your name)

looked back at her sad past again and went on to lead a super

rocking life!

PSYCHO CONFESSIONAL

When my boyfriend dumped me for another woman, I did the only reasonable thing I could think of: I flew to Mexico with a friend and took mushrooms for four days. Unfortunately, I did this without alerting my boss, and since it was midweek during an especially busy time, I returned to find that neither my job nor my boyfriend was waiting for me. So I crawled into bed to sleep off the mushrooms for a few weeks and had the kind of revelation that would only occur to someone heartbroken. The next morning, I went to my ex-boyfriend's office and demanded he give me a job with a bigger salary than the one I'd just been fired from, since it was technically his fault that I'd gone AWOL. At that point, I was escorted out of the building. I currently work in a rehab facility where, if you can imagine this, I was a patient for a while.

Anonymous

Mill Valley, CA

INT. COFFEE SHOP—DAY

Two young, terribly hip women, Delilah and Shay, sit in an über-cool New York coffee shop having coffee and chatting.

                    SHAY

    So then I find out that not only is he
    sleeping with my sister, but he was
    also sleeping with my best friend.

                    DELILAH

    I thought I was your best friend.

                    SHAY

    But he's really a good guy.

                    DELILAH

    Yeah, he sounds great.

                    SHAY

    I mean, yeah, he was always stoned and
    borrowed lots of money and never even
    mentioned paying it back, but he was
    soooooo sweet. I just wish I could get
    him back.

Delilah sits in stunned disbelief.

                    SHAY

    What? He had really soft hands . . .
    and he always shared his cigarettes,

and when he got really drunk he would
stay out all night so as not to dis-
turb me when I was sleeping. That is
soooo thoughtful.

DELILAH

Check, please.

SHAY

Do you think I should call him?

Chapter Six

IF HE WAS SO GREAT, YOU'D STILL BE TOGETHER

He just broke up with you. So really, he's not that great a guy, unless you are just an awful person, which we don't think you are. Or you broke it off with him, so he can't be that great or you would still be together. It's the paradox of a breakup. There seems to be a need to say nice things about the person who just broke your heart, and we get that. You don't want to seem bitter, and you don't want to tell the world that the guy you gave your heart and a large part of your time to is an asshole. Your pride doesn't need the additional blow of having your friends and family think you're a loser for being with him in the first place. It's okay if you don't want to seem petty or knock down someone you once cared about.

HOWEVER, we must warn you that there are two conditions that afflict many refugees of recent breakups. First is what we call **Revisionist Romance Disorder**. RRD, like an acute case of 20/20 Blindsight, creates an inability to see the past as it actually happened. Additionally, those who suffer from Revisionist Romance Disorder cannot control the need to rewrite their relationship to match the feelings they want to have about it. With RRD, an incessant cheater becomes "a really good guy" who was just scared of getting too close. The drunk that forgot your birthday becomes "the one that got away." It's an easily identifiable disease, but like all afflictions, the first step to overcoming it is to admit you have a problem. And your problem is that if you truly want to move on, you need to stop rewriting the past and see your relationship for what it was: the good and the bad, the ups and downs, the baffling, the maddening, and the ridiculous.

To do this, you need to put aside all feelings of embarrassment or shame over how the relationship unfolded—or ended. It's okay to have been disappointed by the fact that he forgot your birthday, or never put forth any effort with your family, or seemed to care more about his work than you. If he's a cheater, it's okay to hate him for it—it's a totally natural reaction to being betrayed. As much as it sucks, you need to force yourself to remember your very worst times together, his most irritating habits, and the hard truth that not only can he live without you but he'd rather. Ouch! Yes, indeed, but doesn't that make it easier to be without him? When you rewrite the past and make your romance seem so perfect (example: He cared so much about my friends that he had sex with one of them; it wasn't that weird that he always called me by his ex-girlfriend's name), your loss starts to seem unbearable. And it's not. Believe us. The demise of this relationship is the result of its not being a fit, a match, meant to be and certainly not the love of a lifetime. You need to stop pretending that it is. Remember, it's called a breakup because it's broken, and who wants to be in a broken relationship? NOT YOU!

The second condition is **Dumper's Remorse**. Dumper's Remorse is different from Revisionist Romance Disorder because it's not about being deluded about what kind of guy he was all along, but rather about second-guessing yourself. With Dumper's Remorse, you've seen the reality, you know he's not the one for you, and you've even been brave enough to do the deed—but then, when you're faced with your first weekend alone, you start second-guessing your decision. (As in: So what if he slept with other girls? He's just social by nature. Did I just throw out the man of my dreams?) All your insecurities about whether you'll ever find the right guy become a breeding ground for Dumper's Remorse and can lead you to make some very bad decisions—like taking him back and wasting even more time in a relationship that's going nowhere. But here's a reality check: Breaking up with someone is really hard to do—it takes a lot of courage to pull the plug on a relationship. And the fact is that you still did it—you fully evaluated the relationship for all the promise and potential that it offered, then decided in no uncertain terms that it wasn't right for you. Trust yourself, because as Oprah says, *doubt* means *don't* every time—and you doubted he was "the one" so strongly that you dumped him!

But Greg, I've Got Questions

But what if it's not his fault?

Dear Greg

I was going out with this really great guy from work. At first it was just a flirtation, but he finally asked me out and we got hot and heavy pretty quickly. Because we work together we kept our relationship a secret. I would have been fine with that, but our boss, not knowing that we were together, asked my boyfriend to take a client's daughter out for dinner and suggested that dating her would help seal a big deal for our company. Long story short, he had to start dating this other woman for work and now he says he's confused about his feelings for me and thinks that we should take a break. What do I do?

Phoebe

Dear Really Great Girl from Work,

Hey, why not just let him throw a sheet over you every time you go out? What a great way to say I love you and I'm ashamed of you at the same time. He may be a really great guy where your boss is concerned, but with regards to you he sucks! Reality check: He did not "have" to start dating this other woman. If he were so great and if he really cared about you, he'd have told the boss he had a girlfriend—he didn't even need to reveal that the girlfriend was you. Let's redefine "Really Great." "Really Great" is proud to go out with you. "Really Great" doesn't hide you behind an office plant. "Really Great" doesn't date other people when he has a

girlfriend, and "Really Great" doesn't let his boss dictate his love life. If I were you, I'd take a "Really Great" break from this not-so-great dude!

But what if he can't break up with his other girlfriend?

Dear Greg

I was going out with this guy for about four months. Every-thing about him is amazing—we have so much in common and the sex is incredible. He's really sweet to my dogs and even will stop by to let them out if I have to work late. I can tell he'll make a great father someday, and I definitely thought we were headed in that direction. UNTIL one night when I surprised him by showing up at his place with Chi-nese takeout and found him at home with his GIRLFRIEND! I thought I was his girlfriend! So he explained that he's really in love with me but they'd been together for so long that he felt like he just couldn't dump her. He promised that he would take care of it and asked me to imagine that if the shoe were on the other foot, wouldn't I want him to let me down gently out of respect for what we'd had together? I agreed but told him that I didn't want to see him until he'd done the deed. So a month has gone by and he still hasn't been able to break up with her because he's just too nice a guy and can't do it. When will his girl-friend realize that he doesn't want to be with her and get the hint?

Alyssa

Dear Delusional,
Normally I would say, "Move on." But this guy is obviously a great
catch because he's sweet to your dogs. In every other way, he's a
total dick. It's so hard to find a man who is nice to dogs, so hang
in there. Or you could WAKE UP! It sounds like his girlfriend isn't
the one who needs to get the hint. She's the one with a boyfriend.
The only thing you should be doing is taking yourself out of this
"nice guy's" lady buffet. You're more than a side dish and deserve
to be treated as the delicious main course that you are. Don't get
me wrong, dog lovers are great, but a guy with a spine and some
values is even better. Nice is in actions, not words. And when you
take a long, realistic look at your situation, or even just reread
your letter to me, you'll realize that you're giving an okay guy who
cheats on his girlfriend a hell of a lot more credit than he deserves.
He's a coward and a betrayer of not one but two women, and he
clearly feels ambivalent about you at best—otherwise, he would
have left this other woman a long time ago.

What if there isn't anyone better out there for me?

Dear Greg

My ex-boyfriend has some really amazing qualities. He's
smart, funny, a total fox, a great dresser, well read, has
great taste in music. He even speaks Spanish, just like me,
which was so great when we went to Pamplona for the run-
ning of the bulls. True, he never wanted to hang out with
my family or my friends (he said my girlfriends bugged
him), which really bothered me—so I broke up with him. I've

been dating again, but haven't met anyone nearly as good.
Do you think I was too harsh? Did I blow it? Did I just throw
away the love of my life? I mean, no one's perfect, right?
Ursula

Dear Urs Case Scenario,
I can't tell if you've made a mistake or are suffering from a case
of Dumper's Remorse. I know that, personally, I couldn't put any
real time in with anyone who didn't like my tribe. My guess is that
you're lonely, and now, when faced with the reality of getting
back into the dating pool, you're panicking. Suddenly, Pamplona
Joe doesn't seem so bad. But you broke it off with him for a rea-
son, and it might be as simple as you just plain weren't in love with
him. After all, the guy doesn't have to be a total asshole for you
to not want to spend the rest of your life with him. Sure, he had
a lot of the qualities you like, but he was missing on some key
fronts. In this case, I'd say "close" or "not quite" is still a big,
resounding "no."

What if he was made to order?

Dear Greg

I finally met the man of my dreams: a doctor who comes
from a great family, loves kids, and treats me like a queen.
He was everything I ever wanted—successful, caring, finan-
cially secure. He was even Jewish, just like me, and my par-
ents were thrilled that I was finally dating a Jewish guy.
And yet we broke up because he figured out that I wasn't
physically attracted to him—I think the fact that I needed

several glasses of wine before we had sex was the giveaway.
But he was perfect, Greg, and now I've blown it over some-
thing I might have been able to change.
Daphne

Dear Let's Not Get Physical,
He may have been made to order and perfect on paper, but the résumé doesn't make the man when it comes to love. He was perfect except for the things that weren't perfect, which makes him ultimately *not perfect*. This is classic Revisionist Romance Disorder—going back and erasing the parts of your relationship that didn't work so you can punish yourself for not marrying him. Listen up: You actually did the right thing! Physical attraction is incredibly important to a long and loving relationship, and if it isn't there at the beginning, I don't have high hopes for it showing up later. Keep looking for a nice Jewish doctor who rocks your world in bed too. Better yet, scrap the résumé and be open to whatever else the universe puts in front of you—because your soul mate just might be a NASCAR driver with a poet's soul who's never even been to a bar mitzvah.

✦ BONUS QUESTION

Should I confront him again now that
my eyes are open?

Dear Greg
My boyfriend broke up with me after three years of what I
thought was an amazing relationship. Even though he said

there was no one else, I suspected that he was lying, so I did what any normal girl would do: I broke into his e-mail and voice mail and did some snooping. Turns out that he'd been seeing a woman from work for the last year that we were together. Nice, huh? I know we're already broken up and it shouldn't matter at this point, but it's completely shaken me and made me question our whole relationship. I want him to know that I know about his infidelities and see him for what he truly is. I can't stand the fact that he thinks he got away with it. How do I confront him about this without having to admit to the snooping?

Andrea

Dear Confrontational,

What a great idea! Go stir things up again with the guy who not only dumped you but also cheated on you for over a year. He sounds like a winner. Just because he clearly had a foot out the door for a while and showed no respect for your feelings or the relationship you shared, why wouldn't you want to reopen and prosecute that case? Oh, maybe because the only thing you'll get from doing that is another dose of rejection with a side order of hurt feelings and anger. Who needs that? NOT YOU! He stinks, and the satisfaction you'll get from busting him for his affair is nothing compared to how far it will set you back emotionally. If anything, finding out that he's a liar and cheater should make getting over him a hell of a lot easier than if you were still holding on to some memory of him as this amazing, perfect guy. So you misjudged his character or he turned out to not have any. Who cares? Wash your hands of this guy for good, 'cause he sounds dirty. Yuck!

A Romantic Revisionist's Guide to Reality

We know it's hard to reconcile how sweet someone was during the initial courtship with how they behaved in the end. Somehow in our minds the early, heady days say more about the person's character than the fact that he cheated, dropped off the map, or was just plain cruel. So many of us find ourselves saying, "But he was so great!" Yes, and the people who got on the *Titanic* thought they were going on a vacation. The truth is, things changed and it's important to remember that they did. No matter how you decide to rewrite your past, here is a list of things that automatically cancel out any previous good behavior. If your ex did any of the following, we forbid you to make excuses for him or use the word "great" about your relationship ever again. You are lucky to be rid of him—no ifs, ands, or buts.

* He cheated on you.
* He belittled you.
* He lied to you.
* He disappeared on you.
* He frequently blew you off.
* He had a Kenny G CD.
* He was abusive.
* He put you down.
* He had a girlfriend.
* He had a boyfriend.

* He stole money.
* He hated your family (assuming you like them).
* He yelled at you in public.
* He was married to someone else.
* He thought *Gigli* was awesome, and not in an ironic way.
* He hated your friends.
* He made out with your friends.
* He never appreciated what a total Hottie you are!

THE *Best* WORST NEWS

The bad news is you've been kidding yourself. The good news is that somewhere deep inside you already know that. It's okay—we've all done it at one time or another. It's a coping mechanism. Who wants to admit, "I'm in love with an asshole" or "This just isn't working?" The dude stunk up the joint, but right now all you can remember are the good times. "But he was such a great guy . . ." Look, he may have been a great guy, perhaps even the best one ever to walk the face of the earth, and that's exactly why he got to hang out with YOU. But being a great guy doesn't mean he was great *for you*. Two great people can get together and have horrible chemistry. Most of the people we've dated are great people—just not when we were dating them. The same can be said for us: We think we're pretty great, but we could probably find others who would disagree. (We're not going to go out of our way to find them, but they are out there.)

Facing up to what your relationship was actually like—not just remembering or rewriting the good parts, but dealing with how it really was between you and realizing that the breakup makes sense on some level—is perhaps the most critical step you can take in the process of moving on. Besides, who are you trying to impress with your revisions? Your friends and family, who probably know the truth anyway? Yourself? You don't need to lie to yourself, especially if you truly love yourself for the totally rocking lady you are. Being honest with yourself won't hurt you—in fact, it's the only way you're going to grow from this experience. Avoiding the truth not only prevents you from learning from your mistakes, it also reinforces the belief that you need to fool yourself to get by. Stop teaching yourself that you can't cope!

So take this golden opportunity and get real about your relationship and what really happened. Sure there were good times; otherwise, neither of you would have stuck around for any meaningful amount of time. But be honest, it wasn't all wine and roses: He never wanted to introduce you to his family, you had to fake too many orgasms, he didn't know who either T. S. Eliot or Elliott Smith was. Admitting that it wasn't great all the time doesn't make it anything less than it was. But being honest about it is liberating. It is in that moment, when you really lay down your cards and see the relationship for what it was, that you'll find the freedom to kick it in the ass and let it go.

WHAT I DID WRONG BY GREG

I definitely suffer from Revisionist Romance Disorder. For a very long time after the breakup, I felt the need to tell everyone how great she was. She hadn't been great, she had been downright awful at times, but to admit that meant I would also have to admit that I had been blind, weak, and willing to show up for her not-so-great treatment. So I used a version of her from the beginning of the relationship where she was all kinds of great. I think I may have even made up qualities she didn't have, or, more to the point, qualities I wasn't able to extract from her. I actively, knowingly lied to myself to keep myself miserable, because admitting the truth made me feel stupid. Isn't that crazy? It looks crazy when I see it written on the page, but I did it. So I understand why it happens, but it sure would have saved me a lot of time and heartache if I'd just gotten down with the fact that we were bad together. When I was ready to stop being such a sad sack and was practicing a program of rigorous honesty, I began to see the relationship as it had really happened. I was able to be pissed at her while also being brutally honest about the fact that I was no picnic to be around either and, more important, that I had kept myself in the game. Suddenly, I wasn't mad at her or me. We were just two people in the wrong relationship. But here is the other part of it. She is a great person. She has many of the qualities I wish she'd had when she was with me. We just didn't bring out those qualities in each other. Thus we didn't work, and that's okay. In fact, my wife is quite pleased about that.

How I Got Through It by Amiira

Rewriting romantic history and re-remembering romantic history are two sides of the same coin. See, I was struck by lightning once. It was the first time I laid eyes on the man who would become my first husband. It was that profound love-at-first-sight thing you hear about but don't think will ever happen to you. It completely rocked me—physically, chemically, emotionally, and spiritually. After meeting him, I called my best friend and said, "I just met the man I'm going to marry." Really. I tell you this because it was that moment, unlike anything I've ever experienced before or since, that feeling of absolute certainty, that kept me believing in and fighting for a relationship that was clearly not good. The warning signs were all there from the beginning, but they were no match for the headrush of new love/lust/hope/conviction. Even the fact that he'd never had a relationship that didn't overlap with his last (including when he started dating me) was eclipsed by my complete belief that he was the perfect man for me.

My unshakable faith that we were meant for each other kept me treading water for years in a relationship that was only consistent in its inconsistency. But I marched on because he was the greatest guy I'd ever known (except for when he wasn't) and I'd never been more certain of anything in my life than I was about him in those first moments of meeting him. And it was the memory of that certainty that ultimately paralyzed me. For years the writing was on the wall, but I couldn't see it or chose not to believe it. All I could see was when things were great, how much fun we had together, and how great he *used* to be. Don't get me wrong—he was and probably still is great. I hope to God he's as great as I gave him credit for and remember him being. But he wasn't great at being married to me. Even when things were pretty good, I carried around a feeling of impending dread. Subconsciously, I think I knew it wasn't going to work, even my body knew it, though I was unable to admit it to myself. I once confessed this feeling of dread to a good friend who had seen us through our ups and downs and knew my "great guy" better than most. He gave me an enlightening piece of advice that went something like this: "Falling in love (or lust) and fear feel a lot alike. They both give you that anxious butterfly feeling in your stomach, a sense of excitement, and a general unease physically and mentally. It's easy to confuse love with fear."

I couldn't believe my ears and didn't want to. He was right and I was an idiot. From the very beginning of our courtship (when he had a girlfriend but I was already in love with him), to the very end of our marriage when I was still hanging on to the memory of days gone by (even though I'm pretty sure he had a girlfriend then, too), I had renamed all the fear as love. It was chewing on those words of advice that made me take a long, hard, and very real look at my relationship for what it was . . . riddled with flaws and nearly over. That's when I finally was able to move on.

AWESOME THOUGHT The right guy is out there right now, wondering when he's going to meet someone like you.

Journeywork Workbook
and Sometimes Cookbook

Time for a "He's Really Great" Reality Check! You'll need to involve one of your closest confidants in this exercise. Call your best friend/confidant (or, better yet, invite them over for brunch) and have them give you the reality version of the following statements. (Feel free to add additional ones that pertain to your own relationship.) DON'T get mad at them if they say something that's hard to hear—they love you, and their job is to help you be brutally honest with yourself so you can get over your RRD and move on! We'll start you off with a few:

Statement: We loved spending time together.

Reality: As long as there wasn't anything else on TV.

Statement: We never disagreed about anything.

Reality: Sure, if I admit to being wrong all the time.

Statement: We had so much in common.

Reality:

Statement: The sex was great.

Reality:

Statement: He looked just like Orlando Bloom.

Reality:

Statement: He was really cool to my friends.

Reality:

Statement: He was smart, funny, and had great taste in music.

Reality:

Statement: I don't even remember why we broke up.

Reality:

Statement: We both wanted kids, dogs, and a minivan.

Reality:

Statement: We never fought about anything.

Reality:

Statement: He always did little things to show me he cared.

Reality:

Statement: He never lied, cheated, or made me feel bad
               about myself.

Reality:

Good job! Now that you and your best friend have completed
this task, it's time to eat! Whip up our "Really Great" Egg Soufflé
and then be amazed at what a fabulous cook you are on top of
all your other awesome qualities.

"Really Great" Egg Soufflé

1 cup grated cheddar or jack cheese
½ cup chopped artichoke hearts (optional)
6 eggs
1 cup sour cream

Like an omelet, you can customize this dish to your liking with any combination of chopped veggies or meats.

Preheat oven to 350°F/180°C. Butter a small (6" × 9" or 8" × 8") baking dish (or casserole dish if you're old-fashioned). Layer grated cheese first, then vegetables (or meats) on the bottom of the baking dish. Beat eggs and sour cream together with hand mixer or vigorously with a whisk. Pour over cheese and vegetable layer. Bake for 30 minutes or until a toothpick comes out clean. Yummy!

☆ You can double this recipe, using a 9" × 13" baking dish and cooking an additional 10 minutes.

PSYCHO CONFESSIONAL

My boyfriend was the greatest guy. Twice a week he would volunteer as an umpire at the Little League games for the Urban Athletic League in our community. I'd never really liked baseball, but since I was so proud of him I decided to go to one of the games to show my support. So one afternoon I made my way over to the Little League field, only to find that no one had ever heard of him and that he had never been a volunteer for them. I was dumbfounded, so I called his best friend's girlfriend and grilled her for information. As it turns out, he was spending his Saturday afternoons with the coed from the frozen yogurt shop we went to! I was so pissed. I took all his belongings from my house, including the clothes I had given him, and cut them into tiny pieces and put it all in a trash bag. Then I drove over to his house and dumped the bag out on his head in front of his weekend "girlfriend." What a great guy!

Anonymous
Charleston, SC

INT. FAMILIAR PLACE—MORNING
CLOSE-UP ON JACK
Jack turns with a surprised look on his face.

                    JACK

    Oh . . . hey, Cathy, you took me by
    surprise.

                    CATHY

    Really? Sorry. You shouldn't be sur-
    prised that this is still one of my
    favorite places too.

                    JACK

    No, I guess you're right. I just didn't
    think you'd still come here after we
    split up.

                    CATHY

    I guess I could say the same thing about
    you. I mean, after all, they are our
    memories, they are our moments . . .

                    JACK

    Yeah, but this is my shower.

Chapter Seven

FANCY MEETING YOU HERE!
(Or, The Art of Premeditated Coincidence)

We've all mastered the art of premeditated coincidence, and right now it's probably looking pretty tempting. But believe us when we say that you won't like what happens when you "bump into him by mistake." Chances are he's not going to suddenly say, "Oh my God, I completely forgot that I'm totally in love with you! How lucky that we ran into each other outside my office." No matter how hot you look. In fact, chances are he'll be with his new girlfriend or, worse, his ex-girlfriend. He's moved on, and you need to move on too.

We know that in the movie version of your life, you run into him looking better than Angelina Jolie in a bikini, and he then torments himself for being an idiot and losing you and devises an elaborate plan to win you back that involves a parachute. We get it and agree that it should happen—and have even *seen* it happen . . . IN THE MOVIES AND ON TELEVISION! Real life isn't like that. When you frequent his neighborhood, coffee shop, or the hallway of his apartment building in hopes of "running into him," he's not going to be stoked to see you—only sorry he didn't take the long way to work. And you will go from being his ex to being his "psycho stalker."

Here's the hard truth: He doesn't want to run into you, no matter how good you're looking these days. No guy says, "Wow, she won't leave me alone and she's so hot!" Most people don't like confrontation, and we're not going to stereotype that statement by adding "especially men," but let's face it . . . especially men. So even if you mastermind the perfect coincidental meeting, nine times out of ten it's not going to go the way you want. More than likely, you'll feel a spectrum of disappointing emotions instead of that satisfaction that you're craving. So stop devising ways for the two of you to cross paths. If you put the same amount of thought and effort into getting over this breakup or meeting someone new, you'd probably be over it by now. His regrets or lack thereof are exactly that—*his*. And that's something even the best little black cocktail dress can't change.

But Greg, I've Got Questions

But what if we still frequent the same places?

Dear Greg

My ex-boyfriend and I had this favorite little coffee shop that we'd meet at on our way to work and hang out at on

the weekends. It's a place by his house that he frequented before we were going out, but I love coffee way more than he does, so I decided that I was keeping the coffee shop when we split. If he doesn't want to see me, then he should find another place to go or pick times that he knows I won't be there. That doesn't really count as trying to run into him, does it?
Sarah

Dear Coffee Achiever,
I'll tell you what. You tell me the name of the place, and I'll meet you there and we can get all caffeinated and stalk your boyfriend together. Because no one, including you, really thinks you're still going there for the coffee. So to answer your question, yes, I think you are trying to run into him. Look, I know the thrill of the great cup of Joe, but I also know the misery of planning little run-ins and having them continue to break your heart. I've got a great idea: Why don't you strike up a new relationship with a new coffee shop? Much like your ex, that coffee shop isn't the only game in town or the only latte you'll love in this lifetime. Remember—breakups give you an opportunity to redesign your life. So let's start with where you get your coffee.

But what if we work together?

Dear Greg

I work in the same office as my ex but on different ends of the actual office space. I have to see him every day, and I'll be damned if I'm not going to look my best every time

I go to any of the common places, like the kitchen, or wear an especially sexy outfit if I'm in a meeting that I know he'll be in. I don't actually try to run into him (I easily could, since I know where he is all day long), but I like to drive him crazy by showing him what he's missing. A few flirtatious f*#k-you outfits to make him squirm aren't out of line, right?

Josie

Dear Pussycat Josie,

I am all for you going to work (Bravo!) and looking your best while you do. But you should be doing it for yourself. The thing is, even if you come to work in nothing but a thong, he already knows what he's missing and he still chose to move on without you. His loss. But here's the thing. I worry that when your hotness doesn't change his mind, you'll stop being hot to yourself and suddenly your work and attitude will suffer. Dress up because it makes *you* feel great and you know you're worth it! Dress up because you know there is someone better out there who will notice you as well.

But what's wrong with letting him know what he's missing?

Dear Greg

Ever since my ex dumped me for a skinnier girl, I've been working out like a crazy woman. I've lost almost twenty pounds and am in better shape than I've ever been. Plus, I dyed my hair blond and got all new clothes. My plan for revenge has always been to show up at the bar where he has

*his "boys' night" looking hotter than ever and then flirt with one of his best friends right in front of him. I've worked really hard on myself and think I deserve the satisfaction of making him question his decision to dump me over a few pounds. And now you're telling me that I shouldn't do it?
Sienna*

Dear The New You,
You're not just working out like a crazy woman—you *are* a crazy woman. And as far as flirting with one of his best friends, there's really no better way to build your self-esteem than to make some innocent third party feel awkward! It sounds like you've gone to great lengths to reinvent yourself. That's great if you're doing it for the right reasons—meaning for yourself rather than as part of a revenge scenario. You have to realize that he didn't dump you over your weight. He dumped you because he wanted to date someone else. Now, if he used your weight as an excuse when he broke up with you, then he stinks on ice and deserves someone as stinky as he. (Which we both know is not you!) However, if *you* are the one who decided your weight was the reason he left you, that's another story. Weight may be the easiest thing to blame for your heartache, but the truth is that he's not the right guy for you. You may have lost twenty pounds and changed your looks, but you're still the same hurt and angry person on the inside that you were before your physical transformation. Whatever the situation, let it go and start transforming your insides to match your outsides. Work on building your self-confidence. You're the whole package at any weight, and anyone who makes you feel any different is a clown (including yourself!).

But what if I want to teach him a lesson?

Dear Greg

I saw my ex and his new girlfriend at the mall a few weeks ago. As it turns out, she works there and he was visiting her at her job, which just happens to be a store that I sometimes go into. Well, now that I know who she is and where she works, I can't stop going there. I've even struck up a friendly conversation with her a few times—about BOYFRIENDS, no less—in hopes of getting information about how serious she and my ex are. I know I shouldn't, but I truly cannot help myself. I'm hoping that someday he'll come by while I'm shopping there and she's helping me, and then the whole thing will explode in his face. Does that make me psychotic or just clever?
Mikaela

Dear It's All Going to Blow Up in Your Sweet Face,
It doesn't make you either, really, but it does make me sad to think that you are spending your time trying to instigate a brokenhearted version of *Punk'd*! Not only will your boyfriend and his new girlfriend think you're crazy, but so will the management of the store and you will be forbidden to shop there. I get it, I know how great the version in your head is, but sadly, the other people involved just don't care enough for it to play out like you think it will, and wasting your time on this scenario will only take you longer to move on. Instead, make a pact with yourself that you are not stalker material and find yourself a healthier pastime. Oh, and the guy you're supposed to be with is across the mall in a better store.

THE *Best* WORST NEWS

The best worst news is that you know where he is right now because you used to go out with him. On Saturday morning, he hits the dry cleaner before his game of pickup basketball, and Monday through Friday he gets his coffee at a quarter to nine at the Starbucks on Fifth and Union. The bad part about that is you may have to battle the temptation to "accidentally" run into him. The good part about that is you can easily steer clear of the hot spots because you want to avoid further heartache and are not a crazy psycho stalker. Right? To be a fly on the wall won't bring you the satisfaction you're looking for. And to be the crazy ex-girlfriend who keeps "showing up" or hiding in the bushes will only chip away another layer of your self-respect. Every time you see him, you only make yourself vulnerable to further heartache. Do you really need further proof that he's getting on with his life without you?

Hey, Sister, if you're intent on chasing down your ex, that means at the very least you're feeling better, dressing better, and getting out of the house. Let's not waste that on someone who's already taken a pass. Keep the focus on yourself for yourself. Wanting someone to regret losing you is not a valid reason for stalking. His regret can be the icing on the cake, but your motivation for self-improvement has to and should always be Y.O.U Otherwise, you run the risk of losing your momentum should things not work out the way you planned in your revenge fantasy. Don't get us wrong—whatever spurs you to make yourself better we applaud . . . but we'll give you a standing ovation if it's the right motivation.

WHAT I DID WRONG BY GREG

As a result of not drinking, I lost weight almost immediately even while knocking back a pint of Ben and Jerry's a night. I was doing that to satisfy the sugar cravings from not drinking. Even so, I lost thirty pounds in five months. My skin cleared up and so did my attitude. I started exercising, I started reading, and I started living. But always in the back of my mind I knew I was doing it for her. "When she sees me, she's gonna lose her shit. She won't believe what she's missing." My life started to take shape. The band I was in broke up, then re-formed without me (which is telling), but it allowed me to focus on my stand-up comedy. I wrote an entire one-man show about the kind of guy I had been trying to be and the kind of guy I actually was. It was called *Mantastic,* and eventually it became an HBO special. So you'd think, well, who needs her? And you'd be right. Yet I was still coming up with reasons to run into her: parties I knew she was going to, events I knew she was going to be at, bands I knew she liked. When I did run into her "accidentally" at one of these events, it would always be the same. "Hey, Greg, you look great! You've met my boyfriend." I was doing all this stuff hoping she'd care, and at the end of the day, she just didn't. At least not in the way I wanted her to. Then a thought occurred to me. "I ought to do this for someone who does care." Can you guess who? That's right. Me.

How I Got Through It by Amiira

After my ex and I broke up, we couldn't help but run into each other. He moved two blocks away, which in New York City means you're bound to still see each other because people walk everywhere and there's a real sense of neighborhood life. Neither of us wanted to change favorite pizza joints, breakfast hangouts, or ATMs. It was fine at first, because we were on good terms and were even going to try to be friends. BUT once I learned that he was seeing someone else and there was a chance I'd run into him with his new lady, it was all I ever thought about. As long as we lived in the same neighborhood, took the same subway line to work, and worked in the same business (which required me to be in places where he was a few times a week), all I could think about was which outfit would really make him regret losing me. As long as we shared all the same friends, I would always run the risk of knowing too much about his new life and being hurt by the new details that surfaced. Furthermore, as long as we still had any joint dealings (in our case, finances and working toward an amicable divorce), it would always be an excuse to contact him and an open door to the past. There was no closure to be had, just jail time in my head. What's he doing? What's he thinking? Does he still love me? Does he love her more? Is he thinking that he made a mistake? It doesn't matter, because the cold hard truth was that he didn't love me enough to want to be with me. It took me a while, but I ultimately realized that I had to physically separate myself from all the things that were keeping me stuck inside my obsessive mind. So one morning I woke up and smelled the coffee, and it smelled an awful lot like "Hey! It's over. He's moved on. Why are you doing this to yourself? Because he's not doing it to you—he's happily ensconced in his new life with his new girlfriend (soon-to-be fiancée, then wife) and totally oblivious to you." I looked at my situation and decided I had to move on—which meant getting out of his world once and for all. So I went to my boss and asked to transfer to my company's Los Angeles office and moved out west a couple of months later.

AWESOME THOUGHT Your new boyfriend isn't standing outside your ex-boyfriend's apartment building, so you shouldn't be either.

SAD PERSON'S
Journeywork Workbook and Sometimes Cookbook

List ten places where you could run into your ex.

1.

2.

3.

4.

5.

6.

7.

8.

9.

10.

Now list ten places you will force yourself to go to instead of those above.

1.

2.

3.

4.

5.

6.

7.

8.

9.

10.

PSYCHO CONFESSIONAL

I ran into him and his new girlfriend at the mall and I looked like total hell. Just awful—stained sweatshirt, the works. I was HORRIFIED, and decided I could not let this be his last memory of me. So I formed a plan: We had lived together briefly, so I went to a post office in a nearby town and mailed myself a package addressed to him. I then called him and left a message saying that I'd received what looked like an important package for him, but that if he didn't come by and get it I would chuck it in the garbage. He scheduled a pickup and I scheduled a blow-out, manicure, and pedicure. Let me just say that I looked GOOOOOOOOD!!!!! "Memory" edited!

Anonymous
Honolulu, HI

INT. THERAPIST'S OFFICE—DAY
CLOSE-UP OF LAYLA
Layla, mid-thirties, forlorn, is clearly lying down.

                    LAYLA

     I still can't figure out why he did it,
     and it's driving me crazy. What do you
     think he's thinking?

                    THERAPIST (V.O.)

     Well, it sounds like he was unhappy in
     the relationship.

                    LAYLA

     He seemed happy. If you had seen us
     together, you would have said that we
     were happy.

                    THERAPIST (V.O.)

     Sometimes people just change their
     minds and there's nothing you can do
     about it.

                    LAYLA

     If I just knew why . . .

                    THERAPIST (V.O.)

     You may never know why.

                    LAYLA

Do you think he's in love with someone else?

                 THERAPIST (V.O.)

I can't answer that for you.

                    LAYLA

Do you think he's hurting the way I am?

Pull back to reveal that Layla is getting a mas-
sage.

                   THERAPIST

Honey, I'm not that kind of therapist.

Chapter Eight
WHAT'S HE THINKING?

By now you know what we're going to say: WHO CARES?! But for those of you who are just *dying* to know: Is he as miserable as you are? Does he miss you? What is he doing? Who is he doing it with? What's he wearing? Does he want to get back together? What are his friends telling him? Is he hooking up with his ex? These are the thoughts that plague you when you can't sleep, can't work, when you're falling asleep at work, and when you're working at not sleeping. We understand that before you can fully get over it, you may need to indulge yourself with a little "what's he going through" obsession.

Here's what you want to hear: "The only reason he hasn't called you is because his debilitating sadness has left him lying on the floor of his apartment in a pizza box full of tears. The only activity he's been able to manage is feverishly planning a way to win your heart back. He's sworn off women (except you), booze, and fun because nothing is fun without you. He may never smile or laugh again." The only true thing in this paragraph is that nothing is fun without you—but even that isn't true for him, because he's going on with his life.

We know you want him to be pining over you and unable to make it through the day. In a perfect world, he's tormenting himself, wondering how he could have made such a mistake, and remembering all the good times you had together. He's barely managing to feed himself and get to work on time, and he couldn't possibly be entertaining the idea of going out or seeing someone new. He should be mourning too, right?

But here's the straight poop. If you've been dumped, the pain is fresh, awful, and unbearable at times. The rug has just been pulled out from under you, and your world has been turned upside down. All those plans you had are gone. Over. Just like that. But the even suckier part is that the one who dumped you has had a huge head start on the healing. However long he entertained ending the relationship is also how long he's been emotionally extracting himself from you. So while your wounds are fresh and ugly, your ex has the advantage of not only being in the power position, but also having had a chance to wean himself off of you emotionally while you have to go cold turkey. It's a harsh reality, but the truth is that he was already partially or even totally over it before you even knew it was going down. And if you've ever been the one to instigate the breakup, then you have a pretty good idea of what he's going through right now. Yes, breaking up with someone sucks. Yes, you do feel badly about hurting someone's feelings. But the fact of the matter is that once you get past the initial guilt, the overwhelming feeling is relief. So if you really want to know what he's thinking, it's probably this: He feels bad about hurting your feelings, he misses you sometimes and even thinks of calling, but ultimately he is relieved that it's over.

But Greg, I've Got Questions

But what if he doesn't realize the mistake he's making?

Dear Greg

There is no way that my ex-boyfriend is ever going to find someone better than me. He even admitted it when he broke up with me. We've been split up for six weeks now and it's driving me crazy. If he already knows that no one will love him the way I do, then what is he doing?

Haley

Dear Best Thing,

He's moving on, pretty lady, but not to join the priesthood. While it may be true that he won't find anyone better than you, it is true that he was most likely only saying that to make you feel better about his imminent departure. We do that sometimes. Statements like "I'll never find anyone better" really mean "I still think you're great, but I want out of this, so please don't cry. I'll get the check." Listen, Hot Stuff, despite his proclamation it looks like he's gonna give it the old college try, so we suggest you do the same and get a master's in Great New Guy.

But what if he's just sabotaging himself?

Dear Greg

My ex-boyfriend and I lived together for nearly three years and have been together for five years total. A few months ago, we got engaged and started planning the wedding. We had the most passionate relationship you could ever imagine and were the envy of all of our single friends. If ever two people were meant to be together, it was us. So you can only imagine how floored I was when out of nowhere he told me he was seeing another woman. Of course, I broke off the engagement and kicked him out, but I think he just got freaked out about getting married and the other woman was merely a way to sabotage things. Even though he's with her now, I know he's not in love with her, so what is he thinking?

Colette

Dear Engaged,

First of all, he wasn't "seeing" another woman—he was having sex with another woman. I "see" women all the time. Those of us with eyes generally do, but it doesn't break up great relationships. Here's what I'm thinking. Actions speak louder than words, and his actions have led him to have a naked party with someone else. If dude is gonna sleep with another girl every time he gets "freaked out," you're better off not signing up for a lifetime of heartbreak and possible STDs. Sadly, he's given you his answer already, so open your eyes to what's actually happening, put on your cross-trainers, and run in the other direction. Remember,

it's called a breakup because it's broken on some level, even if you
didn't know it.

Will I ever stop thinking about him?

Dear Greg

*If I could just get over it, I would. Believe me, I don't like
being stuck in the purgatory of my own obsessive mind. I've
been doing everything right. I've immersed myself in work
and friends, gotten out of the house, tried dating new guys,
joined a gym, and done everything else I can think of to
keep me busy. But it doesn't matter, because the only thing
I ever think about is what he's doing—where he is, who he's
with, how he's getting on. I literally force myself to go
through the motions of my life, and I keep thinking that it'll
get better, but I'm driving myself crazy. Will the time ever
come when I actually stop wondering what he's thinking?*
Victoria

Dear Supergirl,
I can't applaud you enough for doing all the stuff you are doing.
I'm actually standing on a chair in my office giving you a super
kick-ass standing ovation. I promise you that it will get better in
time, but the sucky thing about time is that it takes time. In the
meantime, work on setting realistic emotional goals for yourself.
Try shooting for feeling "different" instead of "amazing," or "less
depressed" instead of "all better," and then see if you aren't
encouraged by your ability to reach these milestones. Once you
accept that it's a slow process, you'll be surprised at how quickly

you heal. And yes, that magic moment will come when it won't even occur to you to think about him, much less what's going through his mind. If you truly cannot cope with the speed in which things are happening, I would advise seeking professional help. I can tell you for a fact it accelerated my own recovery, and it was cool to talk to someone who'd actually been to school to learn how to help me through the rough patches.

But maybe he'll come around.

Dear Greg

My boyfriend and I love each other very much but want different things out of life (I want kids and he doesn't), so we decided to split up. Even though we broke up on friendly terms and the decision was mutual, it's so hard when the problem isn't the lack of love or commitment. I still love him and he loves me, but neither one of us is willing to budge on the kid issue. I thought for sure that when we split up he'd realize that he couldn't stand being without me, and that he'd change his mind about having kids once he got a taste of life alone. I hate being broken up from him, but I want to have children (with him) and feel like if I don't stand my ground I'll always regret it. This has to be torturing him as much as it's torturing me, right?
Samantha

Dear Sammy,
You're right. It completely blows when the downfall of a relationship is not the lack of love or commitment. But the truth, and

clearly you already know this, is that wanting the same things in life is just as important for the survival of the relationship as that love and commitment. Having children is a biggie, and a very personal decision. It's not like the debate is about "what color comforter should we get?" Being a parent myself, I have to tell you that for me having kids is the greatest thing I've ever known, and I would be filled with regret had I not taken a path in life that provided me the opportunity to experience it. That's just me. But if you're feeling like you want that out of life, then you should listen to that voice, because it will only get louder. As for him, he may be tortured over this as well, but he's obviously listening to the beat of his own drummer, and that drummer isn't playing the tune "Let's Make Babies." Better you come to grips with it now and be grateful that you ran into this roadblock sooner rather than later. There are men out there who want to have kids, so hang tough and move your tortured heart on.

But how can he just walk away so easily?

Dear Greg

Michael and I met in college and quickly fell in love. After graduation, we moved to Denver, where we got jobs in sports medicine, and two years later we got married. I thought we were doing great, but then suddenly last fall he decided he didn't want to be married to me anymore. After being together for seven years, he just wants to end it! Thankfully, there are no kids involved, but I'm just destroyed. How can he walk away from our life together so easily?
Kayleigh

Dear Destroyed in Denver,

Walking away from a healthy and fulfilling marriage or long-term relationship is never easy—that's why people stay in them for entire lifetimes. When someone does walk away, it means that they've fallen out of love, for whatever reason, have wanted out for a really long time, and finally got up the courage to do the deed. OR that there is another motivating factor in the equation— like, I'm sorry to say, another woman. Either way, the thing you have to reconcile with yourself is that while you thought things were great, he was working out an exit strategy. What this means is that clearly at some point the two of you stopped being in the same relationship, but he was the only one to notice or take action. So while his leaving might seem sudden or easy to you, it was probably anything but for him. In his mind, things have probably been broken for a while, and what looks easy now is likely the result of many hours, days, and perhaps even months of questioning his own needs and whether a future with you was really the one he wanted.

But doesn't he miss me at all?

Dear Greg

This breakup thing is hard! What makes it even more difficult is that my ex isn't even calling or checking in. The day we broke up is the day he stopped calling. Not even a single e-mail. I mean, if I e-mail or call him, he responds, but he never initiates it. How can we be so close one day and then the next it's as though I don't even exist? I miss him so much! I can't believe he could move on so quickly.

Please tell me he's thinking of me. Doesn't he miss me at all?
Navi

Dear M.I.A.,
Sadly, it sounds like he doesn't miss you—at least not enough to call you. The thing you don't seem to grasp here is that you are broken up. You shouldn't be calling or e-mailing anyway, because your status with each other has changed and contact with him won't help you cut those emotional ties. It's not like he left town on business for a week; he left the relationship for good. And even if he does miss you occasionally, those feelings are superseded by his conviction that the relationship wasn't for him. Even if he is thinking of you, he doesn't want to be in contact with you—which should tell you that the breakup is for real, and that you should leave him alone and move on.

But doesn't he have the same memories?

Dear Greg

I've been in love a few times in my life, but never anything like what my ex-boyfriend and I had together. Our relationship was perfect from the first second we laid eyes on each other up until a few months before we broke up. We did things that most people only dream about: took a year off and traveled the world, got matching tattoos, and built our dream house from the ground up with our bare hands. Before meeting him, I was stuck in a nine-to-five life, so our adventures together really defined who I have become as a woman. Now that we've broken up, there's not one thing that doesn't remind me of him. I really thought that those few months of less-than-perfect was just a phase and not worth throwing away our future over, but obviously he didn't. How can it just be over? When I look back at the life we shared, it makes no sense. Doesn't he have the same memories playing in his head?

Misty

Dear Misty Watercolored Memories,

I'm sure he does have the same memories you have, unless he's recently suffered a traumatic blow to the skull (and I'm not saying that you had anything to do with that, if anyone asks). Even though it sounds like you had a very adventurous and memorable relationship, he clearly had other overriding feelings that carried more weight than those memories. How can it just be over? Because it is. The relationship may have been perfect for you, but it wasn't for him. It's called a breakup because it's broken. That doesn't change or discount the great times you had together. It just means that you need to look elsewhere to make new memories.

> ### But how can he even think about being with someone else?

Dear Greg

I was out with my friends the other night and they let it slip that my ex is dating another girl. It's only been a month!! I couldn't imagine being with someone else so soon; I see

him in every guy I look at. Besides, I was hoping we would
get back together—now how can I be with him after he's
been with someone else? Is he thinking of me when he's
hooking up with her?
Amber

Dear Amber Waves of Pain,
People move on after a breakup—sometimes quickly, sometimes
slowly. The thing you have to remember is that it was over for him
before he ended it, so he had a head start on the process of get-
ting over it. Not only that, but people get over breakups in dif-
ferent ways. Some like to do it alone, and others like to jump right
back into dating. It sounds like you shouldn't be banking on a rec-
onciliation, so it doesn't really matter what he's thinking when
he's hooking up with his new lady. My guess is that since he was
the one to move on, he's not looking back. All you need to know
is that a Superfox like yourself is destined to find a better rela-
tionship—once you let go of this one, that is.

THE *Best* WORST NEWS

The best worst news is that he's probably not pining away for
you—which makes it all the easier to get over him because
HOW DARE HE NOT BE!? It would be unfair to generalize
and say that men don't mourn the loss of relationships; if they
didn't, we wouldn't have singer/songwriters, poets, and the movie
Swingers. But by and large, men do have a tendency to recover
more quickly from the setback of heartbreak. The truth is that

men and women are wired differently and tend to deal with their breakups in different ways. Men seem to be more sexually driven by nature and seek companionship more frequently and less selectively. So while a woman in the midst of heartbreak might not be able to even think of looking at another guy, a man might deal with the loss by getting back on the prowl, or opting for a wet T-shirt contest and a bucket of wings to heal his broken heart and hearty appetite. Men also don't really allow themselves the same indulgences during a breakup as women do, so they are socially conditioned to get past it faster or risk being seen as pathetic. Men are pretty dumb, really.

Think about it this way. Have you ever broken up with someone? Left a job that you were unhappy in? Severed ties with a friendship that you had outgrown? Or cut something out of your life that wasn't working for you? Then you know that on all of those occasions, the common thread was that you were "over it" before you actually got out of it. Being over it is, in part, what pushed you to end it in the first place. If you've been on the receiving end of a breakup, then you have to swallow the bitter pill that your ex is already over it and was possibly getting over it before you even knew you were in it. How much does that suck? What sucks even more is getting hung up on the "what is he thinking and feeling?" shit. Does he miss me as much as I miss him? No. If he did, you'd know it by his actions. Is he seeing someone else? Maybe. Probably. Or at least he's planning on it. Again—it sucks, but if you get real about it you'll realize that knowing the answers to these questions still doesn't change the fact that your relationship didn't make the cut. But—and here's the best news part—as you will learn in the next half

What I Was Thinking BY GREG

Despite my crushing breakup with Ms. New York City, I have on occasion been the dumper. And on those occasions, I usually behaved like your standard guy. After the demise of one particular three-year relationship, I walked out of her apartment and into the courtyard of her building. Was I crying? I wasn't. As unpleasant as the last four hours of breaking off a fairly doomed relationship had been, I was relieved and even a little exhilarated. Would I cry about it later? A bit. Was I sad? At times, but not as sad as she appeared to be. Did I want to get back together? No. Would I want to have sex with her again? Yes. Did I? Once. Was it a mistake? A big one. It only made things cloudy, even though we'd both agreed it was just sex. Did we stay friends right after? Tried to. Did it work? Not at all. What happened? She finally agreed to stop calling and breaking into my voice mail, and I agreed to stop drunk-dialing her. Are we friends today? We e-mail once a year, and she's in a great marriage with kids and everything. What's the lesson here? That all the drama and all the back-and-forth didn't change the fact that we weren't right for each other. Guys may flip-flop and send confusing messages, especially when the potential for sex is involved. But if you really listen, they're telling you everything you need to know by breaking up with you in the first place.

of the book, this breakup could be the event that not only changes your way of thinking about who you are and what you deserve, but also takes you to places you didn't know existed. So again, who cares what he's thinking? You've already given him enough of your precious time.

WHAT I DID WRONG BY GREG

I couldn't shut it off. What's she doing? How can she walk around when I can't even get off the couch? How could we both be in the same relationship and not feel the same way about its demise? Well, I struggled with this last thought for a long time, until one day out of the clear blue sky (and maybe through some pathetic journaling) I realized it was so simple. *We weren't in the same relationship.* Ever. Not from day one at the bar, where we made some weird handshake agreement about going out. I was never in the relationship I wanted to be in. Now, a person with a strong set of standards and a clear idea of what they wanted out of life would have found this relationship unacceptable from the get-go and politely said, "No, thanks." But for a directionless guy with low self-esteem and a flare for drama, it was PERFECTO! *We weren't in the same relationship.* Once I figured that out, all those questions seemed irrelevant, because now they were all answered. But the beauty of it is that now I get to be here on the page with you, so you can hopefully learn from or at least laugh at what I did wrong and not do it yourself. If you don't, that's okay too. Because I'm telling you that from this great fall I've come a long way and I love my life now more than I ever thought possible.

How I Got Through It by Amiira

I spent years wondering, "What's he thinking?" and "How could he do that?"—both when we were together and broken up. It was like an ongoing game of chess that only I was playing. I was sure I could get him back in the game once I figured out what was motivating him and made him realize what he would be losing. I was constantly trying to find the reset button on our relationship to get us back to the place where things were great. Now, I fancy myself a bit of a smarty-pants, but even though I knew logically that you can't coerce someone into feeling what you want them to feel, I wasn't above testing that rule. There's nothing I wanted more than for him to have the same fire burning inside and the desire and will to salvage our marriage. But all my attempts at the mighty wake-up call were glaringly unsuccessful, and he never did spring into action and become the guy that I wanted him to be. Sadly, there was nothing stronger than his ambivalence about our future together. As far as he was concerned, we could stay together or break up. Whatever. It's cool. Is it? As if the choices were even remotely equal. In my version of what my life was supposed to be like, I'd always imagined that my marriage would be something that both parties would feel invested in. Finally, it dawned on me. All of the "What's he thinking?"s and "How could he do that?"s were my own trip—not his. What became crystal clear was that HE WAS NOT THINKING ABOUT IT AT ALL! Only I was! That's why he did the things he did. And he didn't do the things I wanted him to because this didn't even occur to him. Our marriage was that unimportant. It wasn't even on his radar! He was content with the ebb and flow of that which made me miserable. And you know what else I realized? He was not sitting around wondering what I was thinking, feeling, or doing, so why the f*#k was I wasting my time? Sometimes the cold reality is that guys just aren't thinking about us at all. This revelation made it so much easier for me to finally lay down my king and accept the checkmate that had been on the board for so long. Real love doesn't require a strategy—but getting on with your life does.

AWESOME THOUGHT There are a lot of handsome dudes at the gym, and some of them like women.

SAD PERSON'S

Journeywork Workbook and Sometimes Cookbook

Let's throw yourself one kick-ass pity party! It's okay to cry, but crying all day at work is not the way to go, Sister. Look at his picture one last time, smell his old sweater, and then get ready to give it all up, 'cause the healing is about to begin. Start by picking out some appropriate music. You can either pick the saddest CDs you have and put them on "shuffle" or "random" in your stereo—or why not go to town? Download all the saddies from iTunes and burn yourself a Boo Hoo mix. As long as it's a party, there should be snacks, hors d'oeuvres, and a box of wine. How about an outfit? What are you going to wear to your pity party? How about something cozy? Pajamas and big socks are always a big hit in the movies. Now mix yourself up some cookie dough and eat it raw, pausing only to sing melancholy songs into your wooden spoon. A box of tissues isn't a bad idea, either, while you're splurging.

PSYCHO CONFESSIONAL

had been seeing this guy who lived in a different state for the better part of a year. He came into town and we went out on a hot date that started with sex in the bathroom of the super-nice restaurant we were dining in and ended with me asking him to think about moving to New York. I told him that if we didn't live in the same city, I didn't know if I could remain committed to him. He said something along the lines of "Committed to me, what are you talking about? You're not my girlfriend . . . we just have fun together sometimes. . . . You thought you were my girlfriend? Really? You did not . . . you did? Come on, no way. . . . Wow, I am so sorry!" I was SO HUMILIATED! But I was also truly baffled enough to ask him, "How could I not be your girlfriend? We go on vacations together, we have sex, we talk about intimate things on the phone, you call me when you travel, and you come to visit me." He just shrugged and said that I was just one of the people he was dating. I couldn't believe it, so I actually hired a private detective to find out just how many girlfriends he had. And for $5,000 I found out that there were a few of us. But unfortunately, my suffering with this boy didn't end there. Even worse was years later when he invited me to his wedding solo—without a guest—and I went hoping that he'd see me and not go through with it!

Anonymous

New York, NY

Part 2

THE BREAKOVER

(Or, How to Become a Superfox Breakup
Warrior with Lustrous Hair and a Whole
Bunch of Self-Worth!)

With every end comes a beginning (yeah, that old chestnut), and now, at last, here we are at the kick-ass reinvention of YOU! That sounds pretty good, doesn't it? The great thing about life is that you get to choose who you want to be and then take steps to become that person. And you get to start over whenever you want, no matter what mistakes or stumbles lie in the past. So this is where we're going to map out the steps necessary for your total breakover. We've wallowed, we've coped, we've questioned, and we've cried. Now is the time to send Super Sad Sally home and reveal the Superfox breakup warrior within.

A breakup can cost you your happiness, security, confidence, and rationality, as well as your favorite T-shirt and Moby CD. And that's not where you want to be. We know that about you. Think about all of those home-makeover shows you see on TV where the house starts off in shambles. The plumbing doesn't work, the foundation is giving way, and it's just a dirty, sad, and broken place. Then the team comes in and rebuilds it, restores it—they make it a f*#king palace that brings people to their knees. (In a good way, not by hitting them in the legs with a two-by-four.) Even the house itself can't believe what's happened. Well, that house is you. That's what you want to be. You want to burst through this experience with dignity, grace, strength, and a whole new set of windows. "But I never had windows in the first place," you protest. It's an analogy—work with us. The point is, you can emerge from this experience a better version of yourself than you ever dreamed possible. Doesn't that sound awesome, pretty lady? We think so too. It happened for both of us, so let's make it happen for you!

What follows is our list of Breakover Commandments. These are merely suggestions, but we are suggesting them at the top of our lungs. If you follow these commandments step by step, and take advantage of the exercises we offer in our Breakover Superbook, you'll find that you're making progress before you even know it. Reinventing yourself is hard, we know. Putting him out of your mind is even harder. But the only way through the darkness and into the light (where the perfect man of your dreams is waiting, by the way) is to pick yourself up and take action.

Here's the really great story about you: You are fantastic. You are doing the best you can. But we bet that lately, and you might agree, you haven't been doing a whole lot of thinking about you.

Or at least "you" as you pertains to "just you" and not "you and him." If you aren't focusing on you, it ain't gonna happen, baby. So let's take him out of the equation starting today. This is your experience, and from this point on, it should be about *you*, not you and him, or the past. The only way to get to the "reveal" of the new and improved Superfox with the killer set of windows is by continuously moving forward. Our seven commandments will show you how.

The First Commandment
(or, Just a Really Good Idea)

DON'T SEE HIM OR TALK TO HIM FOR SIXTY DAYS

ixty? Yes, sixty. But . . . NO BUTS, PRETTY LADY! We know it seems like a long time, and it is. But if ever there was anyone in need of "he-tox," it's you! (Get it? he + detox . . . aren't we clever?) This is our #1 commandment, and it is hands down the most important thing you can do for yourself. The idea is to get him out of your system—and he's much less likely to continue to wield his power and stay under your skin if you don't have any contact. Furthermore, laying down the sixty-day rule gives you the opportunity to take control of a situation that has you reeling out of control. It's your chance to call the shots. We don't care if he (or you) still wants to be friends, if he still has some of your stuff, or if you were fused together in a welding accident. You can revisit all these issues two months from now when you have some clarity. (And by then you probably won't even really care if you talk to him anymore.) This is about taking care of you, and putting yourself in a position where you can get through this really tough time with some measure of ease.

Sixty days gives you the emotional distance necessary for total recovery. Let's face it—right now your ex is still pushing your buttons. And he will continue to do so until you remove the button. No contact is the easiest way (and possibly the only way) to avoid all the problems and pitfalls mentioned in Part One—the breakup half of the book. "But, guys, it's not that simple." Actually, it is that simple, it's just not that easy. If you were quitting smoking, you wouldn't buy cigarettes, hang out with people who smoked cigarettes, go to places where people were smoking cigarettes, or get drunk and call cigarettes at 4 A.M. begging them to come over for one last smoke. Realistically, the only way to avoid all the little methods you and your ex have for torturing each other—he calls to check in, you make excuses to see him, you obsessively check your messages or, worse, his messages—is to take him out of the picture and cut off all contact.

In our experience, there's something about two months—that's sixty days, 1,440 hours, 86,400 minutes, lots and lots and lots of seconds, or whatever you want to call it—that is magical. *When you get there, you'll know exactly what we mean.* "What if I can't?" you ask. You can. And we know that's the truth, because eventually you will have to. It's only a matter of whether it's your choice now or his choice later, because at some point he will stop taking your calls or meet someone else. One or both of you will finally tire of the long, drawn-out drama. So choose the option that will allow you to feel good about your choices from this day forward. Don't be the cuckoo bananas ex-girlfriend who won't go away. Dive into a self-imposed "he-tox." That means NO

CONTACT! Not only are you not reaching out, you're also not accepting his calls or visits. There is no gray area with this one. Even if you intend on maintaining a friendship with him, take at least a two-month vacation from the relationship. Trust us, if he's truly the kind of friend you want and need, he'll understand— and more than likely, he'll be grateful for a little distance himself.

Still not convinced? Then answer this: Why should you talk to the person who just broke your heart? You wouldn't go back to a job you'd been fired from every day just to feel bad about yourself, would you? "But I really loved my job." So what? They fired you. "But my job was so good in bed." What? This is the part where your job calls security and escorts you out of the building. (And quite honestly, security has better things to do with their day . . . and so do you!)

Try and think of it this way: You're giving the time you were spending on him back to yourself as a gift, and he'll get none of it for at least two months while you set up shop as the new you. You know how you have all of those little tasks and projects you've been meaning to get to? Well, now you've got the time! Whether fun (alphabetizing your ice cream) or horrific (filing your back taxes), these are usually the things that will make you feel better about yourself once you've accomplished them. They can also provide a great opportunity to reconnect with who you are, and start putting energy back into activities and relationships that may have been neglected when you were with your ex. Here are a few ideas:

✳ Reorganize your closet and refold every piece of clothing you have.

✳ Finally put all of your photographs into albums or labeled photo boxes. And while you're at it, make copies of some of your favorite photos of family and friends and send them, along with a note, to the person in the photo.

* Download all your CDs onto your computer or iPod and then sell them back to a used-record store and spend your newfound cash on that Marc Jacobs pencil skirt you've been eyeing.

* Ask a friend to teach you how to knit and then start your own "Stitch and Bitch" knitting night.

* Dust off your clarinet, piano, guitar, or whatever dream is sitting in the corner collecting dust bunnies and give her a whirl.

* Rent your favorite movies from your formative years, and invite some friends over to enjoy your own John Hughes/Cameron Crowe/Quentin Tarantino/Adam Sandler film festival.

* Go to a magazine stand and browse all the titles and see what you're drawn to. You might have a new interest that you didn't even know about.

* Try your hand at gardening. Plant some gardenias under your bedroom window and night-blooming jasmine by your front door so that your home smells like heaven. If you live in an apartment, how about growing a few potted herbs? Nothing livens up your windowsill like rosemary, basil, and thyme.

* If you've got a dog, why not have it trained to be a therapy dog to visit hospitals and brighten other people's days?

* Get certified to be a Big Sister for an underprivileged kid, or volunteer at an outreach center. Now's a perfect time to think about someone else besides yourself. Remember, you have a lot to offer!

How the Hell Am I Supposed to Do That?

Two months can sound really daunting. That's why in many twelve-step programs they do things one day at a time. You can't be in tomorrow; you can only be in today. So today, to the best of your ability, you are not going to see or speak to him. We'll deal with tomorrow, tomorrow. Get it? If you read this tomorrow it will be today, so congratulations on making it on your own for one day so far. You can even mark your calendar each time you make it through the day—there's nothing more inspiring than seeing a row of black shiny X's all lined up.

If you still find yourself strongly resisting this idea, you'll need to take an honest inventory and figure out why it's so hard for you. After all, you know yourself better than anyone—and if you don't, it's high time you did. We even have a place for you to do this inventory. That's right, it's time to get yourself a notebook! "Great, guys, just what I want at this point—homework. I hope there's math." Look, we understand, and really you can do most of what we recommend in your head. But there is something transforming about seeing it on the page and realizing that you put it there. Having actual proof that you are doing work on yourself and a place where you can revisit your thoughts, mark time, and measure your progress is truly affirming. The other great thing about your notebook is it can be a safe place for you to put all the crazy down on paper so that you don't take it out into the world. "What if I want to write in a coffee shop?" Hey, no problem! That's not the kind of "taking it out into the world" we were thinking of (see the Fifth Commandment, page 233).

The Smart Girl's Breakover
SUPER BOOK

Let's start your notebook by giving it a face, or more specifically, HIS face. "I'm not going to cut his face off and put it on a notebook. That would be illegal." Point taken. So instead, find the very best picture of him you have as well as the very worst one. In the front of the notebook, paste the two pictures at the top of the first page. Below the best picture list his best qualities, the things you will miss the most about him, and then complete the following sentence: This is the man who _____. Below the worst picture list his worst qualities, the things that you absolutely will not miss about him, and then complete the following sentence: This is the man who _____. If you're having trouble getting started, we've included a sample of what it should look like.

Best Picture of Him	**Worst Picture of Him**
Best Qualities	*Worst Qualities*
Looks like Ashton Kutcher	Not as smart as Ashton Kutcher
Loyal to his friends	Talks about friends behind their backs
Appreciates beauty	Watches too much porn
Brushes teeth regularly	Always scratching his balls
	Bad taste in footwear
	He cheated on me
	He broke up with me

Things I Will Miss	*Things I Absolutely Won't Miss*
His sense of humor	Dick jokes
Cuddling by the fire	His cuddling with his neighbor
The great sex	Him having sex with the neighbor
The way he looks at me	The way he looks at the neighbor
	His neighbor
This is the man who *I thought I was going to marry.*	This is the man who *f*#ked me over.*

Once you've completed your list, let's take a long look at both sides. Your ex is both of these guys and has all of these qualities. It's so easy to remember only the good things and romanticize the relationship for how it was in the beginning (i.e., perfect), rather than recall how it deteriorated over time and the problems that led to its demise. Now this is the first thing you will see every time you open your notebook. He wasn't perfect. Your relationship wasn't perfect. At the end of the day, he's just a person like you. Except not as pretty, and he scratches his balls a lot. Now turn the page and let's get this party started.

So where were we? Right. Sixty days without seeing or speaking to him and why that's hard. "Because I miss him, you jerks!" We know, and we've heard it all: You're used to talking to him, you're not used to sleeping alone, you really want to salvage the friendship, he hurt you and he's not getting off that easy, he still has your favorite socks, he has your favorite penis, and so on and so forth. They're all just excuses and reasons not to move forward. You're already broken up, and as we've established, he's already way ahead of you in the process of getting over it. So ask yourself what hanging on to or demanding scraps of his attention gets you. What does tormenting yourself (or him) get you? Does the momentary relief of hearing his voice make up for the reinforced rejection you feel when every phone call or meeting doesn't result in your getting your old life together back? What about him is more valuable than making yourself feel whole again?

These are questions that you need to answer, and your notebook is where you're going to do it. In fact, we suggest that every day for these sixty days you write in your notebook first thing in the morning. Even if you have to get up fifteen minutes early and you have nothing to say other than "I have nothing to say," "I really want to call him," or "I hate these bozos who make me write in a journal every day." Grab your coffee and go to town. Just doing it will eventually give you the ability to leave some of your thoughts, pain, and anxiety on the page for at least a few hours. How nice would a big ol' break from thinking about him be? How nice would it be to cut your friends, who've been so supportive, a little slack? We know you feel like crap. We know this sounds like a bunch of "blah blah blah, try this, it's cool" bullshit. If that's the way you feel, write it down. In fact, whenever you have any huge feeling—good or bad—and you have a spare moment, write it in your notebook. Rage on the page! Or just scribble, draw pictures, or trace your hand and make it into a Thanksgiving turkey.

If you're looking for some more specific instructions, try completing the following sentences and just see if they don't turn into rambling paragraphs on their own. You may be surprised by how much stuff is bursting to get out of your head.

1. Sixty days without talking to him is going to be hard because _____.

2. Why should I be the one who has to _____.

3. The time I think of him the most is _____.

4. Today, instead of giving in to the impulse to talk to him, I'm going to _____.

5. Even when I'm feeling my worst, at least I've got _____.

6. This is retarded because _____.

Dude, I Know What You're Thinking   BY GREG

You're thinking, Yeah, but have you done it? Yes. I have journaled, collaged, and decoupaged. I've sent letters to my anger (It did not respond. Typical.), built a voodoo doll out of my fears, and made up a dance to celebrate my uniqueness. Don't think that last bit didn't freak my roommate out. "Hey, dude, what the hell are you doing?" "Oh, I'm dancing to celebrate my uniqueness." "Yeah, could you not do it in the kitchen or in the house, actually?" There isn't a workbook exercise I haven't done or tried. Do they work? I think they do. They help you deal with your problem, and they give you something to do with the negative energy that might otherwise derail you from living your life. We aren't going to ask you to make a papier-mâché hat of your dreams, but we think that the simple act of putting things in writing helps. Get it out of your brain and onto the paper. Truth be told, I'd never written anything before someone recommended journaling, and now look at me. I get to write books where I tell you to journal. Ha! Life is pretty great sometimes.

Special Circumstances

But what if we live together? Have kids together? Own a chinchilla farm upstate together? What if not speaking for sixty days is an honest-to-God impossibility?

Then your contact should be as brief and cordial as possible while you make plans to not live together or sell the chinchilla farm. If there are children involved, then clearly their well-being is paramount and you, being the super classy lady who is unbelievably graceful in trying situations, will rise to the occasion . . . while keeping the contact to a minimum and strictly about the kids. DO NOT use the chinchillas to punish your ex. They are innocent in all of this. Their lives are stressful enough with all the running around and growing of hair. Same goes for the children.

Kids are resilient and can survive a breakup or divorce if it is handled well by the adults. You, being the rocking breakup warrior that you are, have to redefine your relationship with your ex. How you do this will be a big part in teaching your kids about relationships. Clearly, this will be one of the more difficult situations you'll ever face, and you need to negotiate it carefully. Sixty days with limited contact can actually help diffuse some of the tension, and narrowing the focus of that contact to the kids and their well-being will help the redefining process begin. You may make mistakes along the way, but that's just part of the learning curve, so go easy on yourself. How you handle it when you make a mistake is more important than the mistake itself.

Survey Says

The number-one regret stated in the hundreds of breakup surveys we read was "I wish I had just cut off contact with him and not tried to be friends." Nearly everyone agreed that keeping in touch made getting over the breakup much harder. Not only that, but almost everyone who kept in touch was now no longer friendly with their ex, because eventually they chose self-preservation over continued emotional investment in the guy who broke their heart. Or, at the end of the day, they realized that the person just wasn't worth their time. We're not going to say, "We told you so," but perhaps the masses aren't wrong about this one. We're just saying . . .

AND YOU THOUGHT YOUR BREAKUP WAS BAD!

My boyfriend and I were together for nearly four years. We lived together for most of that time and planned on getting married and having kids. His family has always been a mess, and mine, though not perfect, was certainly nowhere near as much of a burden to us. To give you a quick overview of his family—he's got three siblings, all of whom have been arrested for drugs, shoplifting, you name it. When his sister was arrested for drink driving, none of them could afford to bail her out, because his mother doesn't make that much money and my boyfriend had recently quit his job to start his own company (which I provided the financial backing for). Because of their situation, I offered to pay the bail. The family promised to repay me in increments when they could (which to this day has never happened). Then there was his dad, who was serving a three-year jail sentence for an investment scam. His dad's imprisonment was one of the main reasons we were waiting to get engaged, as my boyfriend really wanted his dad to be a part of the celebration.

So finally his dad was set to be released, and the parole board had to approve where his dad was going to live so they could check up on him. Since he'd split from his wife and no one else had room, my boyfriend asked me if his dad could come live with us until his parole officer gave him the okay to get his own place. He stressed that this way we would get the opportunity to build the relationship he wanted us to have. I should mention at this point that we were living in my house, which I'd bought with my own hard-earned money and for which my boyfriend was paying me a small fraction in rent until he got his own company up and running. So in addition to funding his new company, I was paying the entire mortgage and now his dad the ex-con was coming to live with us for three months. But I was thinking that we were on our way to getting married so this was just part of the package.

WRONG. The day—yes, the DAY—that the three months of parole-ordered stay at my house was up, my boyfriend "fell out of love" with me. Wow. I couldn't believe it either. So I got dumped hard after being either a f*#king saint or a doormat all those years. To say that it rocked my world would be an understatement, and it took me a long time to get over it. I cried, sulked, didn't eat, sleep, or think straight for months. My depression was palpable. But I steeled myself, and did not see him or speak to him once he'd moved out of my house. I refused to let myself even go there after the way he and his family had treated me. It was unbelievably hard UNTIL I found out that he'd gotten another girl pregnant (a one-night stand, I might add) four months after dumping me and ended up marrying her on a Thursday afternoon at the courthouse! Can you believe that? Now I consider myself so lucky to have gotten out of that family nightmare so easy. I could have been saddled with the lot of them and a guy that wasn't that great after all!

Carole

Fairfax, VA

GET YOURSELF A BREAKUP BUDDY

hat the hell is that?" you ask. "Some ridiculous 'therapeutic doll' that I'm supposed to yell at and tell my troubles to? Well, I'm not buying." Take it easy there, Hot Pants! While we like to think of ourselves as your breakup buddy, there is nothing like the ear and heart of another live human being to help get you through this tough time. We want to be the ones you turn to when you need help, and in the event that you can't enlist a friend, we hope that reading these pages will help. But having a good friend to call when you're having a moment of weakness, feeling lonely, or about to eat two whole buckets of fried chicken while sitting in your underwear is where it's at!

If you're the type who thinks, "Oh, I don't want to bother anyone with all this," you are so thoughtful—and don't think that it has gone unnoticed. But take it from us: A good friend will be honored that you chose them and more than happy to help you through this difficult time. One of life's pleasures is being able to help a friend in need, and right now that friend is you. "But I can do this on my own." Yes, you can, but why should you? Van Gogh tried that and ended up sending his ear to his ex in a box.

When choosing a Breakup Buddy, there's probably someone who immediately comes to mind. If not, pick someone with at least three of these qualities:

1. Has at least a mild knowledge of your relationship.
2. Is a good listener or is good at pretending they are.
3. Thinks you're the cat's pajamas!
4. Has a cell phone, pager, or other reliable way of being contacted.
5. Lives in close enough proximity to be accessible during emergency breakup meltdowns.
6. Has an hour a day to talk to you should you need them.
7. Has been through a breakup as well.
8. Does not work as a professional clown.

The idea behind getting yourself a Breakup Buddy is simple: A person in distress (you) is not always able to make the best decisions. Sometimes you need someone to walk you through the day and make sure you don't backslide. But as we mentioned in the first part of the book, you can unintentionally end up driving your friends away with your one-sided obsessive need to "talk" about it. That's why, when you approach a friend about being your Breakup Buddy, you forewarn them that for the next sixty days you will be asking them to devote their time, patience, and energy to helping you. The job can be as simple as being the person you call whenever you feel the urge to call your ex, or a surrogate date for dinner and the movies on the weekend. It should also include being the liaison between you and your ex if there is unfinished business or belongings to be exchanged during your "he-tox" phase. They should be someone you can always turn to whenever you don't know what to do with yourself, and above all, they should make sure you don't do anything that compromises your recovery. Like pulling a midnight breaking-and-entering or succumbing to a Baskin-Robbins binge.

How the Hell Am I Supposed to Do That?

Asking for help is always hard for someone who fancies herself a together gal. In fact, it's often easier to unleash your tears and confusion willy-nilly than to simply approach a friend and say, "I need help." But you know what? We weren't put on this planet alone. Sometimes you just have to accept that you don't have all the answers and that you can't fix everything. Plus, most things in life are just better when we are not doing them by ourselves.

The ongoing sting of heartbreak can be a unique and unrelenting beast. Those who have been on the receiving end have an unparalleled sense of empathy and camaraderie for one another. We all have friends who have been there. Quite possibly you were right there with them, box of tissues in hand. So pick up the phone and call that friend. We're telling you they will be glad to help.

So how is this different from bludgeoning all your friends to death with your sad, obsessive patter? Glad you asked! Enlisting a Breakup Buddy is an act of taking control. Instead of allowing your need to vent, complain, and wallow seep into every area of your life and every relationship you have (which will only keep you stuck and miserable), you are limiting yourself to one friend who agrees to help—thus ensuring that you are supported but don't subject others to an endless stream of whining. Having an established agreement also takes away any guilt you may feel about calling that friend for the third time that day. You asked them to stick with you for sixty days—they accepted. They want to be there. So you can pick up the phone when you need to without feeling ashamed or risking your friendships.

The Smart Girl's Breakover SUPER BOOK Climb into that notebook of yours and write down all the times you can think of in the past few years that you wish you had asked for help. After each one, write down why you didn't. Now write down five good reasons why you should ask for help now, even if all five are because we said so. Now write down five reasons why you shouldn't. Now cross out those last five and get yourself a Breakup Buddy.

Dude, I Know What You're Thinking BY GREG

Did I have a Breakup Buddy? By the time I started getting my shit together, I had exhausted almost every friendship I had, with the notable exception of my incredible sister, but she lived in another state. Fortunately, the program I got sober in suggests that you get yourself a sponsor. Which is exactly where we came up with the idea for the Breakup Buddy. I don't know what I would have done without my sponsor. It was such a relief to be able to share my struggle with someone who had been there himself and could reassure me that, with the right kind of thinking, I could overcome my sadness. Look, there is no doubt that this process is going to suck. Just when you start feeling okay, some incident will come at you out of nowhere and—boom— you'll feel like shit again. In those times of weakness, how great would it be to have someone to call, someone who has pledged to rock with you through this painful time? And know this: Amiira and I are thinking about you too. That is why we wrote this book.

Special Circumstances

"But he was my best friend." So was that girl who smelled like egg salad in the third grade, but you don't still need her around, do you? We understand, sometimes you can get so deep into a relationship that you isolate yourself, and then when it's over you suddenly find you are alone. But now's the perfect time to reconnect with some of your old and more understanding friends. You're not the only one who has ever gotten caught up in a relationship and lost touch with people. Just summon up your courage and make the first move. You'll be surprised at how glad your old crew will be to have you back.

"I don't have any close friends." That must have been nice for your boyfriend, being responsible for your entire world. No pressure there. So here's a lesson for the future: Having a good relationship is no substitute for having good friends. A perfect existence includes both. And from our perspective, we say it's time you had some friends, because you are certainly worth it. That said, friendships don't come overnight, so in the meantime why not seek professional help? It's always good to have someone to talk to, especially a person who's dedicated their life to helping others through the bad patches. Who knows, maybe you'll be able to understand why you haven't been able to get close to people other than your boyfriend—and when the time is right, you'll be able to open the door to new friendships.

Survey Says

Almost every single survey we read included the statement "I couldn't have gotten through it without my friends." We heard of gestures that ran the spectrum from calling every day to check in to taking the brokenhearted one on vacation. The one thing every gesture we read about had in common was how deeply you appreciated it. When it comes to breakups, friendships are the best remedy around, so make smart use of yours.

A Note to the Breakup Buddy

So a friend has asked you to be their Breakup Buddy. That's awesome! And you should consider it an honor because basically they've said, "My life is falling to pieces and you are the one person I can turn to." That's got to feel great because really, isn't that what we were put here on this planet to do anyway—help one another? But now you are thinking, "Hmmm. This is a big responsibility. What am I supposed to do? What if I'm not qualified to be a Breakup Buddy?" Listen, all you need to be qualified is a pair of ears and some patience. That's it. But we do have a list of guidelines and thoughts for you to consider during your two months of servitude.

1. It is NOT your job to fix this person. They'll have to do that on their own. What you can do is listen to them, be honest with them and guide them toward making smart choices .. . like not calling.

2. It's okay to set limits. You have a life too and you don't want to be taken advantage of. If one hour on the phone is all you can do, then that's cool. If you can't talk at work—fine. Just let them know when you are available and what to do in case of emergency meltdowns.

3. Make it fun. It's okay to let them sob into your sweater for a while, but then suggest a movie or a concert or maybe just a

(continued on next page)

hike. In fact, say, "Let's walk while we talk." Try not to let them get too sedentary. Your job and their recovery will be much easier if you're out in the world where life's distractions can prove that even the most heartbroken of us can be amused by small dogs, handsome pedestrians, and a great window display.

4. Patience. Patience. Patience. It may take a while for your buddy to get a handle on her new single reality. That's okay. As long as they are doing it in the safe company of you, their Breakup Buddy, and not their ex.

5. Share the wealth. Your experiences, strength, and hope will help guide them out of the darkness and into the light. You may have been through something similar, so share your story and the things you did that helped you get through it. Hearing it from someone else is more comforting than you can imagine.

6. You're a good friend for doing this.

AND YOU THOUGHT YOUR BREAKUP WAS BAD!

My father was always very strict about his beliefs that a woman should not live with a man prior to marriage. So he was less than psyched when I disregarded his wishes and moved in with my boyfriend of over a year. My boyfriend had filed for bankruptcy a few years earlier, so the apartment had to be in my name as well as all of the bills. Plus, because my boyfriend's credit was so bad, he couldn't get his own credit cards or approved to buy a car, even when he did have a job. So I added him to all my credit-card accounts as the additional cardholder and even convinced my dad (who was still not excited to see his daughter living in sin) to sell him one of his old cars he didn't use anymore. At first my boyfriend was really good about only charging things when he needed to, paying off his part of the balance each month, and making car payments to my dad on time. Things were great, and my dad was warming up to him at last.

Well, my boyfriend started smoking a lot of pot and occasionally doing some other drugs (I think it was cocaine), and ended up losing his job. Instead of looking for another one or cutting back on the pot, he decided to become a talent manager. He charged a ton of office, audio, and video equipment to my credit cards and bought himself some new outfits. For months he just spent like crazy, maxing out my cards and not paying for a thing, including his share of the rent and the car payments to my dad. I tried to be supportive of his new career, yet stern about his spending and how it was really messing up my finances. I eventually asked for the credit cards back. His response to this request was to call me a string of profanities. I went and spent the night at my sister's, and the next morning I went back home to find that he had taken everything and disappeared.

I canceled my credit cards but was still saddled with over ten thousand dollars' worth of debt. I was stunned that I had so wildly misjudged what kind of person my now ex-boyfriend was, and I was embarrassed to have to face my family in light of the current situation. But I called my sister, and she rallied my spirits and helped me get through the heartbreak and disappointment as well as work out a plan to deal with the debt. She helped me focus on moving on, and on what I needed to do to both get back on my feet financially and feel good about myself as a person. I ended up moving back home with my dad, whom I also insisted on repaying for the outstanding balance of the car. It took me six years to pay off all the debt that asshole left me, but it was worth it because I did it myself (even though it really sucked). Most important, I learned (the hard way) that love shouldn't be dependent on what you can do for someone. I have a great job, great friends, a very forgiving and loving father, and some savings now. I hear my ex is working at a Banana Republic in Connecticut.

Gabby

Seattle, WA

GET RID OF HIS STUFF AND THE THINGS THAT REMIND YOU OF HIM

ut there are a lot of good memories that go along with that stuff, too." Great, then you'll enjoy them even more when you rediscover his belongings five years down the road. Right now, the priority is to turn your home into recovery central instead of a "But he had the prettiest eyes" torture chamber. The fact is that this process is about getting over him, and all of the things that constantly remind you of the past—photos, clothing, that sappy mixed CD he burned for you—are just a bunch of stuff slowing you down. And you don't have time for it! You need to detach yourself from any and all relationship memorabilia, realize that they're just material stuff, and take them out of your world for a while.

When you're first coming out of a relationship, the primary sensation you feel is loneliness. There's an emptiness or void. It's like being tossed overboard into a cold lake. You're submerged and surrounded by a shocking sensation that you can't just easily shake off. We think that the only way to fight fire is with fire, or more specifically, fight sensation with sensation. So we're going to fight "lonely" with "different" by making your surroundings seem different instead of empty. We say, let's turn this place upside down.

The first thing you need to do is box up all of his belongings immediately, as well as anything else that reminds you of him too much. Be strict about it, but reasonable as well. Let's not pack up all the glasses because he loved orange juice, but the framed pictures of the two of you, his toothbrush and toiletries, and his CDs have to go. Trust us on this one. Especially the Puddle of Mudd. Once you've packed up the souvenir stand from your relationship, it's time to literally get it out of the house. You know what they say—"Out of sight, out of mind." And by clearing out all of the things that remind you of him, you'll be making room for all the great new things to come.

Part two of making your surroundings feel different instead of empty is to rearrange and redecorate. We're not saying you have to go out and spend a bunch of money and buy new stuff. Just move everything around. Maybe paint a wall or two. Put your couch on the other side of the room, change the angle of all the furniture, and hang the pictures or art on different walls. Switch the curtains in the living room and your bedroom. (Do not put tinfoil on your windows—that's the wrong direction.) Get a new set of sheets, move the bed to a different part of the room, and start sleeping on the other side of it. Empty all of your cabinets and drawers and switch things up. We're going for different with a capital D. When you wake up in the middle of the night to use the bathroom, you should bang your knees on something because the path has changed so radically. Which will feel great after the bruising goes down and you've finished cursing us for giving you the idea in the first place. Because by making your surroundings different you are giving yourself new external cues that should provoke different feelings. And anything *different* from lonely or heartbroken is a huge step in the right direction. It's another way of putting the behavior before the feelings, as we discussed in Chapter 3. By embracing the different, you are leading yourself away from the pain. Even if it means getting bruised shins.

How the Hell Am I Supposed to Do That?

First you're going to call your Breakup Buddy for a packing party. Open a bottle of wine or a six-pack of diet Pepsi, order a pizza, pick out a couple of great albums, and make it an event. Make a few different boxes. One for any valuable stuff of his that should be returned (clothes, electronics, etc.), another one with pictures, gifts, and mementos from your time together, and lastly one with stuff to throw away (like his toenail clippers—yuck). Don't throw out his stuff, because as upset as you may be at him, it's best to take the high road. You will feel better about yourself in the long run.

Your Breakup Buddy should be responsible for returning the box of valuables to your ex, because you are still on your sixty-day "he-tox." The box is NOT an excuse to see him—it's just a box. The stuff marked "trash" can go straight outside into the garbage. As for the box that contains all of the memories of your relationship, you're going to tape it up and hand it over to your Breakup Buddy for safekeeping. Your Buddy will hang on to it while you're working through the pain, and also decide when or if you get it back. Remember, your Breakup Buddy loves you and so do we. Now hand over the box! If you are currently without a Breakup Buddy, take the box to your parents. If your parents live out of town, FedEx it to them. Or put it in your garage or a room that gets less traffic. Heck, you can even rent a storage space, dig a hole in the backyard—whatever. Just get rid of it.

The Smart Girl's Breakover
SUPER
BOOK

Once you've gotten rid of all of those pesky reminders of him and rearranged your space, take a moment. Sit down with your notebook and survey your new surroundings. Write down your first impressions of your new space. How does it look? How does it make you feel? Does your knee still hurt from banging it in the middle of the night? Do you feel a sense of accomplishment and the feeling of having done something good for yourself? You should! Write down your feelings about the way you want your life to unfold starting at this very moment. But here's the key: Your surroundings should tell you that you're already living your new and different life.

Dude, I Know What You're Thinking BY GREG

After my breakup, some new friends and I were talking over coffee one day. The topic was "What's the corniest cliché that you actually live by?" Mine was "No pain, no gain" or some dumb variation on that, because I was still in the process of working through the remnants of my heartbreak. But then Doug, an ex–football player/sometimes actor/full-time bartender buddy of mine, said, "Messy bed, messy head." Really? Messy bed, messy head? Is that Dr. Seuss? We all laughed about it, but sure as shit, the next day I looked down at my futon as I was leaving and thought, "Messy bed, messy head." It hit me like a ton of bricks. The chaos of my unmade bed, my bedroom—and my apartment, for that matter—was directly related to the chaos in my head. It was like I was standing in my unmade brain. The unpaid bills, the dirty clothes, the extra stuff I'd been lugging from apartment to apartment. Clothes I was never going to wear—and all *her* stuff. I had lots of her stuff. When I'm into someone, I like to have things of theirs to remind me of them, especially since I travel and like to have pictures or something to take with me. But having her stuff around postbreakup wasn't comforting—it was painful. Even sweaters of mine that she had worn a lot . . . it was all too much.

Then I did the weirdest thing. I started throwing everything on the floor. It was time to deal with all this crap. I emptied drawers and boxes. I pulled things off shelves and out of closets. I guess I figured if it was on the floor I'd actually have to do something about it.

Forty-five minutes later, everything I owned was on the floor of my apartment. EVERYTHING. Then I went out, got some boxes and some garbage bags. Well, I'm sure you can guess what I did next. "Set up the boxes in a row and played trains?" No. Well, yes, but then I got serious. I started downsizing. I started getting rid of stuff I wasn't using. I got rid of clothes I always said I was gonna wear in the future but never did, magazines I'd kept because I liked one picture of Gwen Stefani, or because of some other reason I didn't remember anymore. I wanted some clarity. I found tons of things I didn't even know I had, which meant I wasn't going to miss it when I got rid of it. The stuff I didn't throw out I organized. I kept a box of keepsakes from our relationship, and another for her stuff that I was going to give back to her. I took a good long look at myself, got rid of the things that didn't serve me, kept the things that did, but more important, made room for the great new things to come. Those things included a career, a girlfriend, and some really nice shirts.

Special Circumstances

"What if we live together?" Well, then, your packing party can be twofold now, can't it? When it comes to divvying up your stuff as a couple, our philosophy is "take what you need and leave the rest." We know that for the purposes of revenge it feels like you should take everything in order to hurt the person who broke your heart. It's certainly something that crosses one's mind and at the time seems like a good way to say f*#k you. But taking everything will only keep you surrounded by things that remind you of him and your old life. It's like sentencing yourself to a mental jail term. It may not seem like it now, but believe us—it's liberating to walk away with as little as possible and start over fresh. Let him have all the baggage!

Boxing Day

I t's really up to you what goes and what stays, but it will only benefit you to be brutally honest with yourself about what artifacts trigger your feelings. Here's a list to help get you started.

Return to Sender (His Box)

1. His CDs. How often are you going to listen to Staind, anyway?

2. His iPod, laptop, digital camera, or any other item of value. Unless he owes you money, in which case eBay is a fine alternative.

3. All of his clothes, even his perfectly worn-in Rage Against The Machine tour T-shirt that you like to sleep in.

4. The baby photo his mom gave you or any heirloom on loan from his family's estate.

5. The engagement ring.

Keepsakes for Pete's Sake (Your Box)

1. Photos, love letters, and birthday cards. It's always great to have memories of the good times. We assume they were good times, as people rarely take photos during a fight. The letters and cards can be fun to read later on, so tie these up in a bow and mark this bundle "Do not open until I've been married for fifteen years!"

(continued on next page)

2. All other jewelry and gifts. You gave back the engagement ring—you're entitled to the other benefits of the job.

3. The videotape of the two of you having sex. Don't want that ending up on the Internet or as the halftime entertainment at his next Super Bowl party.

4. Any and all potential blackmail material, just in case he's not a gentleman after all. Example: the photo of him grabbing a stripper's breast at his brother's bachelor party in Vegas.

5. Anything he made you. After all, he did make the effort of going to Color Me Mine.

Straight-Up Trash (Sayonara!)

1. His toothbrush, razor, retainer, and Rogaine. All evidence that he used to sleep over.

2. His porn.

3. His underwear and socks. These don't really count as clothes, as far as we're concerned. Besides, he's lucky to be getting his other stuff back.

4. His free weights, protein powder, muscle-mass supplements, and stack of *Men's Health* magazines from his two-week-long fitness kick.

5. His Palm Pilot or address book. Oops! Sorry about that.

Survey Says

"Everything reminds me of him. Every song on the radio, every show on TV, every meat loaf, every ATM, every place I go . . ." We can't tell you how often this theme came up in our breakup surveys. If we could wrap our arms around you and give you a pat on the back and a gentle "I know," we would—because we do. We were you once upon a time. If everything reminds you of him, the best way to overcome that is to change your surroundings. If your surroundings are different, you'll *feel* different, and that's good.

Admit it: Every time you look at that photo of you and him, it's like an electric jolt of pain. So stop the masochism! Live by the dictum of "No unnecessary pain," and create a landscape for your life that makes you feel great.

AND YOU THOUGHT YOUR BREAKUP WAS BAD!

A few years out of college, I met a dashing European photographer and fell madly in love. We traveled the world, quickly became engaged, and decided to split our time between his residence in Italy and the States. We got married in Italy and spent our first six months there. Then we found a great apartment in the Village in New York City. We were living the life. He was working on a book and was traveling a lot, so he would often go away for months at a time while I started to carve out my own career. As our living situation was international, I couldn't take a steady job, but I didn't care because we were talking about starting a family soon and he wanted me to travel with him more, so a traditional job would have made that impossible. After 9/11 and as our first anniversary approached, he suggested we move to Los Angeles. So while he went to Italy for a few months, I moved to L.A. to find us a house. We didn't spend our first anniversary together, or my birthday, which was two months later. When I had to have an emergency medical procedure, it wasn't my husband that flew to be by my side, it was my dad. I overlooked my husband's absence, because he was working on deadline and he was so far away. But it seemed like his plans to come join me in L.A. were always being postponed.

Finally, it got to be four months since we had seen each other. I finally told him he had to come out or I was coming there, because this was not how I had imagined my newlywed life to be. He agreed and flew out later that week. We lined up a dozen prospective houses to look at and went car-shopping. We decided on a house and bought a car. Then he told me he didn't want to be married. He had no interest in couples counseling or seeing if perhaps living in the same country would help our marriage. He'd found out that he liked being alone, something I wish he had investigated before we walked down the aisle and I gave up a few years of my life to be with him. The divorce was quick and the entire situation puzzling. Strangely, my devastation was short-lived, probably because we'd already been apart for four months, which made it less of a shock. So I moved on with my life and put my Ivy League degree to good use and got a job that I was excited about. I started dating again, and who do you think showed up in my driveway on my birthday the next year wanting to give it another try? I told him to pop the trunk while I just got a few things together. Then I took the boxes of his stuff that had been filling my front closet and loaded up his trunk and sent him on his way! He was completely dumbfounded, and I had a great birthday.

Nina

Los Angeles, CA

GET YOUR ASS IN MOTION
EVERY DAY

W hy do you have to bring my ass into it?" Because it's time to get it in gear. Let's face it, one of the side effects of a breakup is an abundance of new-found time that if not used properly can become your downfall. You need momentum to move through the breakup process, and the only way to keep yourself in motion is to first get yourself in motion. To start, we're going to recommend that you just get out of the house every day. Remember the Sun? Take yourself on a walk, take your broken heart to the movies, or simply get in the car and drive. Just get moving. When you're surrounded by empty hours that used to be filled by your relationship, it's actually easier to be unmotivated than to get fired up about all the cool new ways you can fill your days. People tend to become introverts when they are wounded, and the natural response is to hole up and feel sorry for yourself. But the key to turning your breakup into a breakover is to fight the inertia by taking an opposite action. When you feel the urge to crawl into bed, you need to call a friend and make a plan that forces you to get out of the house. Instead of sitting around feeling sad and broken, you want to be doing something that makes you feel strong and resilient again. This is where physical activity comes in.

You want to be a breakup warrior, so why not try something that makes you feel tough, like kickboxing or martial arts? Have you ever glimpsed your reflection in a wall full of mirrors throwing a roundhouse kick and a couple of jabs? Talk about empowering! Or how about yoga? It looks like a relaxing class in stretching, but get halfway through one session and you'll think you've joined the Marines. It feels great to do something challenging, especially when you've spent the previous day watching TV from under the covers. You need to turn yourself back on, both literally and figuratively, and getting a jolt of physical energy is a great place to start.

Each day that you take care of you is a small victory, and that's what we're shooting for here. Don't want to try kickboxing or yoga? Fine. We say go to yoga not because everybody's doing it, but because you've been feeling really bad lately and we want you to do something that makes your body feel *good*. Hell, hate the class, skip the class, whatever—just get yourself there and then blow it off, if that's what makes you feel better. The simple act of having someplace to be, of making a plan and then following through, will do wonders for your sense of purpose.

Your "breakover" doesn't have to involve exercise, but we can tell you that it's one of the best ways to jump-start your healing process. When you exercise, you not only feel strong and accomplished, but your thoughts will become clearer and more focused. You'll stop the obsessive brain loops of "why, why, why?" if you're focused on biking that next quarter mile. You'll work out all the physical tension and stress that's probably got you wound up so tight. It's one of the few things in life that really feel like rebuilding—plus it makes you look better! You'll clear your pores, move the blood through your veins, and maybe even trim a little sadness off your waistline. If hitting the gym isn't for you, that's okay too, just pick something outside the walls of your house (like tanning—at least you went outside!) and, as we said . . . get your ass in motion. Shake it, stir it, just get it moving and out the door!

How the Hell Am I Supposed to Do That?

Don't set goals that are too lofty, and don't get down on yourself. Make them small and make them attainable. We're not saying that you're going to feel great right away, because creating momentum from stillness takes both work and time. Make a pact with yourself, write up and sign a contract, or just put this book down right now and go outside, walk down the street, and grab a cup of coffee. Decide that you are going to do something every day that makes you feel stronger, better, and gets you out into the world. Make a list of places to go, things to do, people to see, errands to run, art exhibits to attend (it could happen), rock shows and movies you want to check out, or go dancing or take a cooking, knitting, or tae kwon do class. Then pick one every day and do it. Remember, this is your time, and you get to do whatever you want with it, so spend it creatively. Follow your whims and instincts—as long as they don't pull you back onto the couch.

Take a moment now to think about the kind of relationship you'd like to have the next time around. Ideally, it will be well-rounded and filled with activities that you enjoy, experiences that enrich you and ultimately make you a better person. Now go and have that relationship with yourself, Hot Stuff. Besides, you've got to have a life, because when you do meet the next guy and he asks you what you're into, you don't want to say, "My ex-boyfriend."

The Smart Girl's Breakover SUPER BOOK Get out your notebook (groan) and take an honest inventory of all the things you let slide during your relationship. All the things you blew off, didn't make time for, couldn't do because your ex didn't want to, and so on. Put them in the order of importance that they should be completed in . . . then scrap that and do the ones that seem the most fun first.

Dude, I Know What You're Thinking BY GREG

I couldn't walk a mile. I'm not kidding you. When I finally decided to turn the poor-pitiful-me disaster that was my life around and head for Happyville, I weighed 227 pounds. I was fat, tired, and way out of shape. My goal: to button my pants so I didn't always have to wear my shirts out. I wasn't going for a Brad Pitt Fight Club physique—I just wanted to be able to breathe while I was going up the stairs to my room. After months of thinking about it, I finally got all jocked up in my sweats and started out my front door. "Couple of miles should do the trick,"

I thought. "Today I become a runner." Well, I hit the wall about a block and a half from my house. It was a disaster. My lungs felt like they were bleeding, I was seeing spots, and I thought lactic acid was gonna shoot out of my legs. I wanted to cry. I was thirty-three years old and I couldn't run a hundred yards. But something weird happened in that moment. I just kept going forward. I walked and I walked and I walked. And then, the next day, I walked again and then again and again and again. And soon I would walk and jog, and then I would just jog, and then I started running. I never had a plan when I left the house. I never had a distance or a time. I had no goal other than to leave my house in my sweats. And return. I guess that was a goal too.

Special Circumstances

"My job keeps me really busy and I barely have time for anything outside of it. Doesn't going to work count as 'getting in motion'?" That depends. Does your job enrich your life? Do you feel stronger and more accomplished from doing it every day? Are you moving through the pain of your breakup, or are you simply delaying dealing with it because of a heavy workload? If you can't do something moderately active every day, if your schedule absolutely prohibits it, then set more attainable goals. How about the weekends? Can you dedicate some time for yourself on Saturdays? Nights? Bank holidays? This is about you forcing yourself to take time out to honor YOU. Obviously, the more time you put in, the more you'll get out of it. Jobs are certainly important, but you are your priority right now, so make a little time when you can.

Survey Says

Keep yourself busy! That's what everyone says helped get them through their own personal Vietnam. Of course, an overwhelming number of those surveyed listed recreational drinking as the most prominent activity. We won't condemn event drinking, but would like to take the stance that we think there are better ways to gain the needed perspective and momentum. As we've discussed, the perspective you get from tequila is often skewed, and it doesn't necessarily make you feel better about yourself the morning after. But exercise was a close second and offered the twofold reward of feeling accomplished and looking hot. That's more like it, ladies! Many also took their breakup as an opportunity to reevaluate their lives and ended up making big career changes as a result. Others discovered new hobbies and activities, like surfing, vegan cooking, and landscaping. One fine entrepreneurial gal even started her own scrapbooking company. And two others we know used their experience, strength, and hope to put together this little book. (Us.)

AND YOU THOUGHT YOUR BREAKUP WAS BAD!

My boyfriend asked me to go on vacation with him after we had been together for about six months. Things were great and this seemed like a big step, so I was very excited about it. We researched tropical locations and talked to travel agents and ultimately decided on Cancún for our first trip as a couple. We planned it a few months in advance, and as our vacation approached, he said the magic "I love you and I want to spend the rest of my life with you" phrase. His friends who'd said he'd never be the marrying kind were now eating their words and congratulating me on being the one to bring the eternal bachelor to his knees. I was madly in love and couldn't wait to go on a romantic vacation with my future husband.

So the week before we're meant to leave for Cancún, I ran into his ex-girlfriend, whom I had met a few times before, as they were still friends. "Ran into" is actually the wrong term, as she clearly had called my office and found out where I was having lunch. She purposefully came right up to me, handed me an envelope, and said, "Well, I guess you won." I had no idea what she was talking about, but I opened the envelope and found airline tickets for her and my boyfriend and an all-inclusive package for the very same vacation he and I were going on the next week. She calmly explained that he had been trying to decide which one of us he wanted to be with and had planned identical vacations with us both. I was stunned, but she seemed to have not only known about it from the start but also been confident that *she* would be getting back together with him and going on the trip. I called my boyfriend and confronted him about it, and he used the "I was confused" defense and convinced me that it was a temporary lapse of reason and that I was the one. He wasn't used to having good things in his life and was prone to sabotaging relationships. Like a complete sucker, I forgave him and went on vacation with him a week later.

We had a great time and got our relationship back on track. Months later, he officially proposed and I accepted. We hadn't started planning the wedding yet when his ex-girlfriend of duplicate-vacation fame tracked me down again to let me know that they had been seeing each other and sleeping together again! I was crushed, but even more than that, I was pissed. I told her that she could come by my office to pick up the ring, because not only was she more suited to wear it and deal with his bullshit, but she clearly wanted it. And you know what? She came by and got the ring! I don't know if they ever officially got back together, but I moved on, starting with getting myself away from the bizarre love triangle I had somehow gotten involved in and continuing with a number of activities I hadn't tried before. Some of them were great, like mountain climbing, and some didn't take, like ballroom dancing. The one that was the most enjoyable was volunteering at the Y, because while I was helping out in my community, I also met a like-minded soul who was honest, loyal, and monogamous, and we have a great life with two kids now. Sometimes I can't believe what I almost settled for!

Lydia

Nashville, TN

The Fifth Commandment
(Or, Food for Thought)

DON'T WEAR YOUR BREAKUP OUT INTO THE WORLD

ell, what am I supposed to wear, then?" A shirt, pants, or maybe a nice skirt is always a safe bet. Or how about some confidence? Confidence always looks good with everything. It is our opinion that when you walk out into the world, how you present yourself is a projection of what your life looks like—what your head looks like. If your life is in shambles and you're depressed beyond belief, it's natural to not care about how you look. Why should you, anyway? Life has become an abundance of all-consuming sadness, which eclipses everything else, right? Wrong. Take off your victim pants. What you've got going for you is that you are a superhero in the breakup stratosphere who is in the process of reinventing herself. In this time of crisis and pain, you want to lean into the future where you are whole, healed, and the most rocking version of you that anyone (including you) has ever seen.

Not wearing your breakup into the world means no more public breakdowns or tantrums. No more crying at your desk, shouting into your cell phone, or fighting with your ex at restaurants while you finalize the demise of your union. Don't be the lady whose life spills onto everyone in her wake. Indulging in messy public breakup behavior only makes those around you uncomfortable and makes you seem unstable. So keep it to yourself and your dearest friends after business hours, and make a pact with yourself to try to live the vision of what you want your life to look like. Every time you step outside, you should make an effort to reflect the person you are on your way to becoming, not the shell of the shattered woman he dumped. Turn that husk into a tamale!

Our rule of thumb is to never leave the house wearing something that you wouldn't want to run into your ex in. That goes for dirty sweats and walking the dog outfits too. We're not saying that you have to dress up for every occasion and put on a full face of makeup—just that your exterior should reflect the metamorphosis that's happening inside. Besides, they make really cool sweats and supercute dog-walking attire these days (that's why the designers for Juicy Couture are billionaires!). What better excuse do you need to finally go through your closet and get rid of all the things you don't wear, can't fit into, or that are never going to come back in style? Remember, a "breakover" is about you feeling confident about yourself as much as possible. Why would you put on something that made you feel anything less than that?

When you see someone who is well-put-together, or exceedingly cool or fashionable, don't you find yourself wondering what their life is like? Their home? Their car? Their friends? When you appear put-together, you project the vibe of being a happening person, which you are. Once again, it's about putting the behavior before the feeling. By dressing in a way that makes you feel really hot, you project the confidence and togetherness that you are working toward. This breakup and recovery period are a slump, not a lifestyle choice, and should be treated as such. Don't dive further into the pit of despair by dressing the part of the sad girl who got dumped (unless you're going to go all the way and open a clothing store called Dumped!, full of baggy and unfortunate clothing). It's a fact that if you look good you're more likely to feel good. So set yourself up to win! Blow people's minds with how well you wear this time of transition. We know you may not believe it now, but this breakup is the best thing that ever happened to you because he was not "The One." So why not dress for the occasion? Because let's face it, revenge is a dish best served HOT! And the best revenge is living well, feeling good about yourself, and projecting those feelings out into the world.

How the Hell Am I Supposed to Do That?

This may be the easiest breakover commandment to actually implement into your everyday life. It doesn't take that much self-control to set boundaries for your grieving process that are as simple as "I'm not going to lose my shit in public today and I'm going to wear something that makes me look good." Considering that in the previous pages we've asked you to move bigger mountains, this should be a piece of cake. You have a closet full of better outfits than that of a volatile depressive, so pick one!

Still wondering how you're going to project confidence and togetherness when your world is crumbling? Our question is "How can you not?" You are all you've got right now, so take actions that make you feel great. Even if your staples are jeans, flip-flops, and a T-shirt, make them your favorite jeans that make your ass look good and your cutest T-shirt that brightens your eyes. Get a new haircut, go to the makeup counter at your local department store, get a mini makeover and buy yourself a new lip gloss, dive into the world of contacts or Lasiks, get some new sunglasses, and put a smile on your face when you strut your stuff, because you are a breakup warrior who is even impressing the hell out of herself! We said it before and we'll say it again—*set yourself up to win*. Keep the "After" photo of your breakover in your mind's eye, and be the gal who provokes people to remark, "Losing that boyfriend looks like the best thing that's ever happened to her!"

The Smart Girl's Breakover SUPER BOOK Grab that handy dandy notebook, a pair of scissors, some tape or paste, and all the magazines on your coffee table and around your house. Cut out pictures of things, people, or fashions that inspire you and tape or paste them into your notebook. Maybe even make a note next to each picture about why you find it inspiring. "Great, do you want me to decoupage a picture frame next? Or should I draw a smiley face on the back of my hand?" Only if you want to. The point of this exercise is that when you open your notebook every morning to write, you will be reminded of the super-hot greatness you aspire to. And perhaps by constantly seeing these images you'll be inspired to make choices and take actions that move you closer to your goal.

Dude, I Know What You're Thinking BY GREG

I always loved style, but I never really had any, probably because all my money went into extracurricular activities or her. Plus I went through my breakup during "Grunge," so it was okay to look like you just got kicked out of Alice In Chains. I realized pretty quickly that it was time for a change, especially if I was ever going to meet someone else. It takes a while to change your physical appearance—remember, I was working on the running—but you can get new clothes today. So I went shopping. I didn't have a lot of coin, so I hit the thrift stores and the sales. While I was shopping, I found I was having a hard time because I had all these dos and don'ts about what I could or should wear. Myths I'd created about what I looked good in and what I didn't, which pretty much left me with a black T-shirt, jeans, and motorcycle boots. I don't know what I had against long-sleeve shirts, they never did me any harm . . . except the one that punched my sister. But once again, I realized that my old way of doing things wasn't getting me anywhere. So I bought a couple of long-sleeve shirts (I know what you're thinking—"Risk-taker!"). And I'm not lying—just wearing a long-sleeve shirt out one night made people take notice. "Hey, you look great," an old friend said. "You must be feeling better." I was about to say, "No, I'm just wearing a long-sleeve shirt," except suddenly I *did* feel better. The fact that someone thought I *looked* better actually made me *feel* better. Truly, I remember that moment because it was the first time since the breakup that I had actually felt good about myself. I was finally heading in the other direction, away from the pain. "Yeah, I feel great" is how I responded. And you know what? I still have that shirt. I even wash it. In fact, it's one of my wife's favorites, so it must be cool.

Special Circumstances

"What if I already dress cute all the time?" "What if I gained a few pounds and none of my favorite clothes fit?" "What if I don't have a torso?" Well, then you need to adapt as best you can. If you're already pulling out all of the stops, then raise the bar. Dig out your good jewelry and put it into everyday rotation, or get your hair cut and highlighted—do something a little different that makes you feel good and look good. If you're in between sizes, then buy yourself some cute sweats and haul your cookies to the gym. If you can look cute while you're doing something proactive, we promise it'll make you feel that much better. If you don't believe us, put on your schlubbiest clothes, dab on some pimple cream, and go to the grocery store. Are you really going to try to convince us that it doesn't make a difference? Don't start your days in the hole. Besides, you never know when the new Mr. Right will come along. . . .

Survey Says

There are two ways to get through the pain of a breakup. You can wait it out or ride it out. Waiting it out means just that—

literally soaking in it, sometimes for years, until it finally passes and doesn't hurt as much. (Nothing more fun than marinating in suffering.) Riding it out is the opposite. Riding it out is when you strap on your suit, grab your long board, and force yourself to get on the wave. In survey after survey, the stories revealed that those who forced themselves to push through the rough waters got through it feeling empowered and confident about their abilities to navigate relationships in the future. Those who waited it out were seething with resentment for the wasted years of their lives and were still wrestling with confusion. I know it's still a hard choice—seething or confident, seething or confident? How about them apples? Sprucing yourself up is the epitome of riding it out. It's a shitty journey, but at least you're gonna look hot on the way.

AND YOU THOUGHT YOUR
BREAKUP WAS BAD!

My fiancé and I were high school sweethearts, together for more than twelve years. His lips were the only man's I'd ever kissed, so you can do the math on what else of his was the only man's I'd ever . . . We'd basically grown up together and had had this complete storybook relationship. He was a part of my family, I was a part of his, and our families had literally become one since we'd been together so long and lived in the same town. We had planned a pretty big wedding (150 people), and had chosen a reception hall within walking distance of the church so that we could lead a processional from the service to the reception. Everything was perfect, and my fiancé and I couldn't wait to be man and wife.

The week before the wedding, he started acting weird, asking me if we really needed the formality of being married since we already were married in his eyes. I thought it was just a case of the jitters and didn't think much of it. There were many dinners and gatherings the week of the wedding, as people from out of town arrived and I got to meet his extended family (fourth and fifth cousins by marriage, etc.). There was one cousin in particular who was super flirty with him, and he with her. Clearly, there was some sort of childhood crush between them, and while the week of our wedding wasn't really the time for it to resurface, there they were, locking eyes, sharing glances, and kicking each other under the table like kids. Whatever, I thought—they're family.

So our rehearsal at the church went smoothly and he and his groomsmen headed over to the rehearsal dinner while my bridesmaids and I decided to make the walk to the reception hall to see how far it was by foot and whether I'd need to have backup "walking" shoes for the big day. Me, my sister, and my closest friends walked the route arm in arm, marveling that I was less than twenty-four hours away from being married. When we got there, I had to pee because we'd been drinking some champagne on the way over, so we went looking for the lounge, which we found . . . along with my fiancé and his fifth cousin having sex! Needless to say, our families aren't close any longer.

Everyone in our town heard about the demise of our wedding plans—it was actually all anyone talked about for months—and I was humiliated beyond belief. At first I didn't even leave the house, because everywhere I went, people were talking about me, staring at me, pitying me. Then something inside me snapped back. I don't know what happened, but suddenly I could see it from everyone else's perspective and I didn't want to be pitied. I wanted to be the girl whom people admired for bouncing back. When I took a step back and looked at my situation, I could see that it was almost funny how ludicrous my life had turned out. It was laughable, so that's what I did—I laughed. Instead of crying, I laughed my ass off. And when I ran into people who were talking about me or offering their condolences, I just laughed it off with a "Better to find out now instead of at the family reunion, right?" It felt great, because as funny as that line was, that's truly how I will always feel.

Tabitha

Ontario, Canada

The Sixth Commandment
(Hear Our Plea!)

NO BACKSLIDING!

Starting over is hard. Starting over again is even harder. So you can imagine how hard it is to start over again and again, and again. That's why we say, "No backsliding!" Backsliding with your ex stops your progress right in its tracks and sends you reeling back into the hellish pit of pain that you've been trying to claw your way out of. It's like reopening a wound that had already started to heal.

What is considered backsliding? It can be something as little as calling to catch up (on how much you miss him) to the Big Kahuna of backsliding—breakup sex—and everything in between. Basically, any kind of contact outside the parameters of your sixty-day "he-tox" rule. While it's not the end of the world, backsliding will rapidly undo all the hard work you've done and progress you've made. Ultimately—though it might feel good during the first few seconds that you see him/talk to him/start unbuttoning his pants—it will only serve to mess you up and make you feel like poo.

It's always tempting for both parties to revisit the crime scene, especially when you're in the very unsteady waters of the first month postbreakup. You miss him, you long for him, you'll do anything to see him. Maybe he misses you too, even though he has no intention of getting back together. Before you know it, you've concocted some lame excuse to drop by his place, like returning his can opener (he can buy a new one, you know), and you end up naked on his kitchen table. Resisting this over-whelming urge is exactly what your Breakup Buddy is for—he or she needs to be on deck to coach you through your weaker moments and prevent you from doing yourself more harm.

When you backslide, you move farther away from your breakover goals, which should be getting to a better place where you feel strong, resilient, optimistic, and whole again. Backslid-ing not only gives you an instant refresher course in heartache but also makes the situation unnecessarily cloudy. And guess what? There's nothing cloudy about it: You're still not right together, you're still broken up, and he's still moving on. We can't emphasis this point enough—IT'S NOT WORTH IT! So try at all costs not to let yourself slide back down this slippery slope.

"But what if I do backslide?" Then get back up on the horse, cowgirl. You didn't break the law, you didn't kick a puppy, but you did do something that should hurt somewhat, and that is you let yourself down. You know you're better than that, and now you know how backsliding feels—kind of yucky, right? So we're cool, just don't do it again. Start over at day one of the sixty-day "he-tox" and see if you don't do better this time around.

How the Hell Am I Supposed to Do That?

One day at a time, pretty lady, by taking it one day at a time. The temptation to check in with your ex, meet up for coffee, accidentally run into him, or succumb to a booty call because you're both lonely is going to haunt you on a daily basis. But these urges are just ghosts from your relationship—bad suggestions from the voice in your head that is addicted to the past. Trust us when we say that backsliding is a mistake that will set you farther back than you can even imagine. Once you give in to it, you find yourself caught in the worst kind of relationship purgatory—the demotion—because you are in effect telling your ex that he can still have access to you WITHOUT the emotional responsibilities. Backsliding doesn't mean you're getting back together, it just means you've lowered your standards and accepted a demotion from ex-girlfriend with self-esteem to ex-girlfriend whom he can still get busy with if he wants to. Backsliding says, "You can have me with no strings attached." Backsliding says, "My self-worth is still in your hands." Backsliding says, "It's okay if you don't want to be my boyfriend anymore. I'll take any scraps you'll give me." That doesn't sound like you, now, does it? We didn't think so. So how the hell are you supposed to avoid doing it? You just have to. Period. That's why those sixty days without contact are so important!

The Smart Girl's Breakover
**SUPER
BOOK**

Take this book over to the photocopier at your office/the library/Kinko's, enlarge the calendar you see on page 248 by 300 percent, and make a few copies. Fill in the dates and mark every day you've gone without backsliding. When you get to sixty days, reward yourself with a spa treatment or something great that honors your person. Now mark every day you've gone without thinking about backsliding other than when you're marking your calendar. When you get to thirty days, buy yourself something special. You're a badass breakup warrior!

Dude, I Know What You're Thinking BY GREG

How could something that feels so good be so bad? Well, isn't that true of all vices? "But Greg, calling him would feel so good right now." Until you hang up and realize that despite your charming banter, you're still broken up. Look, I know it's hard when only days ago you were allowed to touch him, share secrets with him, laugh with him, and even see him naked, and now suddenly it's over. But actually, doing these things with him when it's over is far, far worse. So don't see him. It's too much to take when he is sitting across from you in a coffee shop rambling on about his life that now doesn't include you anymore. Every word, every look, every gesture is a reminder that he is no longer yours. It's flat-out torture. Trust me, I've done it. I've met exes for coffee in hopes of getting back together, and it only made me feel like shit. I've had breakup sex in hopes of getting back together, and the only thing it led to was confusion and more heartbreak. Take a cue from the dictionary definition: Backsliding is going backwards. So if you need company, call your Breakup Buddy. If you get horny . . . well, you figure it out. Just don't call your ex.

Special Circumstances

Didn't you hear us? We are saying there are no loopholes, so don't look for them. You can certainly work together, live in the same apartment complex, follow the same rock band from town to town, or belong to the same credit union without engaging socially or romantically. Unless you are both actors and work in the adult film industry . . . then you are screwed.

Survey Says

This is going to blow you away, but almost everyone in our survey agreed that the best course of action was to *not* see or sleep with their exes! There is not one person who volunteered that backsliding actually helped them move on. And even if there had been, we wouldn't have told you about them. So don't do it, pretty lady!

Sunday	Monday	Tuesday	Wednesday	Thursday	Friday	Saturday

AND YOU THOUGHT YOUR BREAKUP WAS BAD!

My boyfriend and I went out for two and a half great years. We fell for each other instantly, and our relationship was not only the best I'd ever had, but the envy of all of our friends as well. But after two and a half years had gone by, I started pressing him to set a date for our wedding. At first it was no big deal, but then I noticed that he was really reluctant to nail it down. So after a few too many drinks at a friend's wedding, I told him that either he set a date that very instant or I was through with him. He called my bluff, so I ripped the engagement ring off my finger and shoved it into the frosting of his piece of wedding cake, thinking it would have a dramatic effect on him. Well, it did, because after that night he refused to give me back the ring and no longer referred to me as his fiancée. When I told him I wasn't about to be demoted from fiancée to girlfriend, he broke up with me altogether. I was crushed and really thought I had blown it with the perfect guy.

Instead of walking away and sticking to my guns, I found myself groveling for him to take me back. I called him incessantly, e-mailed him, dropped by his house unannounced, ran into him on purpose, and often slept with him in hopes of winning him back and making him remember what we had together. But even though he was all too happy to have me in his bed, he wasn't giving me back the title of girlfriend, much less fiancée. So I had gone from being his fiancée to being a booty call, and I blamed myself for setting this whole nightmare in motion. Then, to top it off, I found out that he was also actively dating, sleeping around, and enjoying his freedom while I was eagerly humiliating myself on a weekly basis. I was devastated and had never felt so low about myself—I was even too ashamed to call him on his bad behavior.

Finally, my best friend begged me to stop seeing him. She'd been trying to get me away from him for a while, but she finally said something that really resonated with me at last—that if he was the love of my life or the man who deserved to be my husband, he would NEVER have allowed me to reduce myself to this pathetic sex toy that I had become. I was floored. At first I was angry and insulted, but deep down I knew she was right, and I cried for weeks. I cried for the loss of my fiancé, I cried for the loss of the future I thought we'd share. But mostly I cried because I was mortified by what I had become—a desperate woman throwing herself at a man I had clearly misjudged. After I mourned, I picked myself up, took my best friend to a day spa, and thanked her profusely for her intervention. I quit my ex cold turkey and now, a year and a half later, I'm doing better than ever. I hear he's engaged again; apparently, he proposed to this woman on their fifth date, which I've taken as a sign that he was meant for someone else. As for me, I've learned that nobody is worth giving up your dignity for and have since met a great guy who inspires me to be a better person, and loves me most when I'm at my highest and not my lowest!

Rochelle

New Zealand

The Seventh Commandment
(And This One Is Non-Negotiable)

IT WON'T WORK UNLESS YOU ARE NUMBER ONE!

You are the prize, the sun, the moon, and the stars. Not him or anyone else. You can love your friends, you can love your family, and you can love every stray dog or stray drummer that crosses your path. HOWEVER, you have to learn how to love yourself, like yourself, and put yourself first before you will ever find the healthy, loving, and lasting relationship you're looking for. Being number one means you can take care of yourself when no one else will, because there are times in our lives when we are all we have, and knowing that we can get through those times is not only reassuring but (we think) a really attractive quality. People love to help one another, but no one has time to carry you. And you don't want to be carried. If you take anything away from this book, it should be that you are defined by how you live your life, not whom you live it with, and certainly not by what you give up to be with that person.

So what does it mean to really love yourself? Above all else, loving yourself means that you feel complete when you're on your own. Not only is that an extremely gratifying place to be emotionally, but it's also a very alluring quality when it comes to romantic relationships. People don't feel like they have to be responsible for your life, because you are responsible for yourself. There's not a needy factor that puts too much pressure on another person. You'll come to your next relationship as equals who expect and bring out the best in each other. "So is that what men want, someone who loves themselves?" you ask. Who cares? It's time to figure out what *you* want. Loving yourself and feeling complete isn't about catching a man—that's an added bonus that comes later. Your emotional growth and well-being should start with you, not someone else, and it should be *for* you, not someone else.

If you ever sat down with Amiira and me, we would tell you that part of the reason we ended up together is that we'd learned so much from all of our past relationships and breakups. We'd been knocked around enough that the idea of being alone seemed better than compromising again. And we'd both done a lot of work on ourselves. Not just the "I lost weight, do I look good in these pants?" variety, but the "Why do I end up in these shitty relationships?" kind. The kind where you try to look at your problems objectively and figure out what part you played in them, even if your part was just routinely showing up for a bad time. The cool thing about this kind of perspective is that it keeps you from being the victim. Victims blame others. But if you recognize the part you played, you can do something in the future to not get involved in a similar kind of situation, or at least see it for what it is before it's too late. So right now, it's time to take a closer look at you and take some responsibility. Not just for the things you might have done wrong, but also the things you've been doing right for so long that you—or he—refused to acknowledge. One of the great joys in life is getting to a place where you really actually like yourself. Not the idea of who you think you are, or who you want to become, but the imperfect, awesome, living soul reading this sentence right now. The only way to do any of this is by exploring you. I know that sounds corny and kind of dirty, but it is meant to inspire.

How the Hell Am I Supposed to Do That?

You're doing it right now. You're currently participating just by reading this book. It means you are taking an action, looking for answers, moving away from the pain and in the right direction. You are a seeker. You have what many don't—the willingness to look, the willingness to listen, and the willingness to learn. That's half the battle, kiddo. So stop right there and applaud yourself, since we're not there to give you the standing ovation you deserve. Unless you're in a bookstore, which might be embarrassing . . . also, why haven't you bought the book? If you've come this far in the book—even if you've only processed some of what we've said—you are still taking action and are hopefully starting to feel better about yourself, the breakup, and your future. Great accomplishments take time but are always worth the effort. Finding a way to love yourself isn't going to happen overnight but realize this: The part of you that got you to read this book is the part that loves you, so you know it exists. Listen to that voice, because it wants you to win.

If you've actually done the things we've recommended, like cutting off all contact, packing away his stuff, and actively doing things that make you feel strong and accomplished every day, then you're probably well on your way to a full recovery and will make a great Breakup Buddy yourself someday. Bravo to you, Superfox Breakup Warrior! Keep on doing what you're doing!

The Smart Girl's Breakover SUPER BOOK Get it out. You heard us. Flip open that notebook that you've been writing, scribbling, and making collages in. Pick a clean, fresh page in the book and paste the very hottest picture you have of yourself right in the middle of it. Around the picture you're going to draw your new Superfox Breakup Warrior Royal Crest. Pick your favorite colors and draw things that represent who you are and what you want out of life. Paste pictures from your life, magazines, or whatever. Make it colorful, joyous, strong, punk, pop, loving, and awesome. "Okay, that's it, that's the last straw. You guys are ridiculous! Do you want me to make a cape, too, and run around saying, 'Look! I'm a Superfox and I'm getting over my breakup!'?" Hey, not a bad idea. C'mon, you've come this far. It's not like we're asking you to share your work with your office mates, so ask yourself: Why are you afraid to do this? Who's cooler than you? Nobody. You know why? Because you don't care what others think and you deserve to see a tribute to yourself! (And also because we're not there to make one for you.)

On the next page or on the back of the page with your new crest, write down the following statement: "Here are the great things that I already know about myself: I am stronger than I thought I was. I am resilient and buoyant in the face of emotional adversity. I am also buoyant in water. The best investment I can make is in myself. I feel good about myself every day." Keep going with as many things as you can think of, and finish with "Let's face it, I rock!"

Now make a list of what you want—not just in a guy, but for yourself in life. Make it as detailed as you can. Now place one hand over your heart and repeat the following statement aloud:

> *I promise to make a firm commitment to living and breathing my list every day, in every relationship, friendship, job, and experience that comes my way, from here to eternity and three weeks beyond that.*

Dude, I Know What You're Thinking BY GREG

One day I opened my notebook and drew a complete blank. I wasn't feeling bad; in fact, I was feeling great and didn't want to trivialize it with my dumb words in my stupid notebook. (Which is just me editing myself and not the point of journaling.) Anyway, I still wanted to communicate something, so I started drawing what ended up being a kind of crest. It was like a shield with a heart and then two guitars crossed skull-and-bones style, and at the top a crown. Very dude. It was total high school notebook style, but it was exactly the way I felt. Then I made a banner and wrote the words "Honor, Dignity, and Grace" surrounding it. Goofy, right? That's what I thought—until I found myself looking at it every time I was in the shitter. It was as though there was this code I was beholden to. I actually created a life with words I believed in, because, trust me, I hadn't been living my life with honor, dignity, and grace before, and now they had become the stronghold of my belief system. Will this work for you? I want it to. But more than drawing a crest or cutting out pictures, I want you to discover that you've come through this crazy, messed-up situation with new words and ideas that you will live by. And hopefully, you will do whatever it takes to remind yourself of this on a daily basis.

Special Circumstances

Oh no you don't! There are no special circumstances with this one, Pretty Lady. There is no situation that is better served by your not realizing that you are the best thing going. Got it?

Survey Says

The most inspiring thing about our surveys was hearing from the people who not only learned from their horrible breakups but found in them the opportunity and need for personal change. A Superfox from Kansas said her breakup actually inspired her to evaluate all the relationships in her life. She found that she was making many of the same mistakes when it came to picking friends and that it was time to stop surrounding herself with people who took her for granted. Another Breakup Warrior wrote to us that after her breakup she did some major "headcleaning" and found that not only had she been holding on to a bad relationship but also some friendships that she had outgrown and a job she was no longer challenged or inspired by. She cut the deadweight in her life—the friends who were too difficult and the job that had no future—and started making choices that were worthy of the person she was. One especially wise woman real-ized what kind of example she was setting for her daughter with her relationship and subsequent breakup. "How can I expect my daughter to find a healthy and loving relationship when, as her role model, I have been settling for infidelity and disrespect as well as acting like an insecure lunatic?!" This revelation caused her to completely shift gears and turn her life around.

AND YOU THOUGHT YOUR
BREAKUP WAS BAD!

I was married for a few years to a guy who I thought was "the one," although he showed me constantly that, even though he was my husband, he really was just not that into me by all accounts. So after years of slugging it out, I finally accepted the truth that it was time to move on. Getting divorced was not really in my master plan, and although it was an amicable split, I was still wildly heartbroken. Though I marched on with my life and jumped into another relationship within a year, it took me years to really get over my ex-husband—and even more time on top of that before he was flushed from my system completely. Unfortunately, during this time I continued to be in relationships that I didn't have the emotional capacity to be in. Not only had I not learned from the previous mistakes, it seemed like I was testing their validity by making them again. Whether it was two dates, two months, or two years, I always ended up dating the same guy.

I finally decided to try dating casually instead of having a boyfriend who I wasn't suited for. It seemed like a revolutionary idea at the time. So I was "casually" dating a few different bozos, each of whom constantly displayed red flags as well as some pretty lame qualities. There was the guy who pursued me who had a girlfriend that he "wasn't in love with but couldn't break up with," so he'd ask me to meet him out somewhere so that technically it wouldn't be a date. What a catch! There was the guy who called me twice a day, took me out to fancy dinners, and then dazzled me with stories of his drug-addled past and how he'd bedded hundreds of women, including his past girlfriend's best friends and sisters. Gross! Still, I managed to go out with him half a dozen times. There were others I could barely sit through one date with. But the amazing thing was that this time around I not only recognized the red flags from the start, but I didn't overlook them or let other, better qualities eclipse them. Believe it or not, this was a HUGE step for me!

Then one day I actually recognized that a fantastic man had appeared in my life. (Another HUGE step!) For the first time, I was blown away by someone's great qualities instead of their dangerous ones. When we started dating, everything seemed effortless, and together we felt like we could literally do anything. Our relationship was buoyant and inspiring and pushed each of us to become an even better version of our individual selves. It was a long journey, but I'd finally found "the one," and now I get to live the most unbelievably blissful life. I'm married to a man who makes me howl with laughter every day and is the best husband I could ever wish for. We have two astonishing daughters who are (no offense) the most perfect people I've ever had the pleasure of knowing. And I'm even writing this book that you are reading now. I wish you the same magnificence in your life.

Amiira

Burbank, CA

FOR THOSE ABOUT TO ROCK

*I*n the end, only you can make you happy. "Really? Why didn't you just put that at the beginning of the book?" Because there is no one-sentence cure for the common or uncommon breakup, even if it is a really good sentence. The only thing we know for sure is that this bummer of an event can actually be life-changing. It was for both of us. Hopefully you'll look back at this breakup and be thankful for it when you're living your kick-ass life with the right person who makes you an even bigger superstar than you already are.

The suggestions in the book are exactly that, suggestions. (But we think they're really good ones, which is why we've offered them to you.) We are not doctors or therapists, just people like you who wanted to share our own experiences going through the same pain. The one thing we really want to stress is that you try to go easy on yourself. Let's say you start the sixty-day plan and then you slip and see him after two weeks. So what? Big deal. Start over. You don't want to start a journal? Don't. But if you feel after a while that you are not getting better, give it a shot. What do you have to lose? And if it all gets to be too much, please go and see a professional. We've been there and we don't care how you get through it—just that you do get through it in the end. The Superfox you were always meant to be is waiting to come shining through—she's just been buried under all this crap that you have to let go of.

The ultimate goal of our book is to help you to make changes in your life and yourself so that you will be available and ready for the RIGHT relationship. Here's what we know for sure: Every relationship you ever have won't work out . . . until you find the one that does. And when you do find "the one," the difference between that relationship and the others you've had before will be profound beyond belief. Good luck and take care of you.

Love from your Breakup Buddies,
Greg and Amiira

Bonus Chapter

DUDE, GET OFF HER LAWN

(The Tough Guy's Breakup Buddy)

We've been told that guys don't really buy these kinds of books. Men process breakups differently perhaps. They get drunk, stand on your lawn, scream at football players on TV, and maybe even start a band. Yet I would have really dug a book like this when I was hurting to keep me from losing my shit. Well, if you are a guy and you are reading this right now, you must be in some real pain, 'cause THIS IS A GIRL'S BOOK! Ha ha, just kidding. We wrote it with women in mind, but the steps we would recommend are exactly the same. Dude, I've been through it; that's how I knew how to write about it. But just in case you don't want to walk up to the counter and buy *The Smart Girl's Breakup Buddy*, why don't we give you the Cliffs Notes and see if that don't help some?

RULE #1: SHE'S NOT COMING BACK!

That's got to be your mind-set or you are not going to get through this. "What about when I camp out on her lawn like they do in the movies?" Bro, it's an awesome image, but as we told the ladies: In the real world, the guy who camps out on her lawn gets arrested. You will be glad you adopted this attitude early on. The only power you have in this situation is to disengage. I'm talking cold turkey for two months! That means no talking to her, seeing her, or sleeping with her. Seriously? Yes, strangely, sleeping with your ex seems to drag out the pain. Weird, huh?

RULE #2: PUT DOWN THE BEER BONG

You don't have to tell me about the sweet joys of getting f★#ked up to ease the pain of a nasty breakup. Those first shots of tequila really do the trick . . . until you're standing outside her window watching her make out with her new boyfriend. Look, we all love comfort food, whether it's whiskey, ice cream (yes, men do it too), or a tasty adult feature (which you should not eat). But excessive use of any of these things just keeps you from going through the pain. Dude, it's going to hurt. Let it. Greet the pain. Say, "Hello, pain. I realize we have business, you and I, but don't get comfortable, because you're not staying." Try to honor yourself during this crappy time. The rule of thumb is, don't put it in your body if it will make you a sad fatty or get you into a fistfight with a tree. Tree wins every time.

RULE #3: GET YOURSELF A BREAKUP BUDDY

"What? Really? Call another guy and ask him to hang out with me while I'm all sad and shit? Are you nuts?" Nuts? No. Serious? Yes. It's better than getting arrested for breaking into her place and going through her underwear drawer. Remember that scene in *Swingers*★ when Ron Livingston comes over to Jon Favreau's apartment with orange juice and salami in an effort to get him back into the world? That's what a Breakup Buddy is. Someone to check in on you to make sure you don't blow it or fall off the face of the earth, someone to give your cell phone to when you slip up and drink all of Manhattan. Someone who will return her stuff or pick up yours so you don't have to, and someone to remind you that this too shall pass.

RULE #4: WALK IT OFF, CHAMP

A breakup is a prime opportunity to, well . . . be a man about it, Hot Shot. Wish I had heeded those words myself. I have very few regrets about my life, but man I wish I'd had some dignity during the sad-sack days. I know it's hard. There are few things worse than the feeling you get when someone isn't into you. Especially when at some point they were. It feels like you've been punched in the gut, and it's hard to motivate to do anything. Don't waste away at the PlayStation eating Cool Ranch Doritos. Take an opposite action. If your impulse is to sleep all day

★If you haven't seen Jon Favreau's *Swingers,* featuring the always-awesome Vince Vaughn, rent it. It's like a chick flick for dudes.

and blow off work, do the opposite. Get up early, take a walk or a run, eat a healthy breakfast, and then blow off work. You get what I mean. You've got to get into action. Exercise is key. I don't know why it's so hard to do sometimes, but every time I do it I feel better. Every time! It doesn't have to be a huge workout, you can just jog around the block, but do something every day. You are not going to let this thing beat you.

THE *Best* WORST NEWS

All I can say is that getting my heart pummeled by a girl who wasn't into me may have been the event that saved my life. As detailed in the rest of the book, I was on the fast track to Nowheresville, and I was taking the tequila with me. It looked like I was going to let the sadness kill me until the morning I woke up and realized, "I can start over. It's my life, and I'll be damned if I'm going to let a stupid breakup ruin me." Have you heard the saying "Whatever doesn't kill you makes you stronger"? They're right. I turned the breakup back on itself and crushed it. You can do the same. Remember, time actually takes time, but you will get through this. Do it with dignity, man.

Take It from a Lady Who Knows
by Amiira

I've played on both teams in the Breakup Bowl. Clearly, the Dumpers are always the winning team; they clean the field with the Dumpees every year. But when the dust settles and the teams shake hands after the game, no one feels victorious. So even though you're suffering, take solace in the fact that she doesn't feel good about that. You can revisit the first part of this book to get a glimpse of how I dealt with heartbreak. As for when I was the one to call it off? Well, that's an entirely different beast.

When you're the one to call off a relationship, there's always a sense of relief when you finally get up the guts to do it. But then one of two things happens: Either the guy takes his lumps and goes away, which leaves you to wonder how he's doing and recast the story of your breakup—the version in which he's a hell of a guy whom you'll really miss and you look back on your time together fondly. When you run into him again months later, you'll strangely be attracted to him.

Then there's the guy who won't accept the bad news. He plays hot potato with the breakup, constantly throwing it back in your hands and refusing to go away. He's the one your friends will forever hate and refer to as "The Crazy Ex-Boyfriend." When you run into him again, years after the restraining order, there's no attraction—just the memory of his bad behavior.

I've had both types of breakups, and I urge you, if it is at all possible, to be the guy who walks away with dignity. Even if you go cry in your pillow for a month and break every plate in the house, just do it privately or in the company of your Breakup Buddy. You'll be thankful that you did in the long run.

I had a boyfriend who was one of those best-friends-where-the-line-gets-blurry-and-next-thing-you-know-he's-your-boyfriend boyfriends. He had many great qualities and we were great as friends, but ultimately we struggled in a romantic relationship. We weren't a match, and so instead of hurting his feelings and breaking up with him, I pulled away until he dumped me. I got out of the relationship, but it was HIS idea—something I had passively-aggressively orchestrated and was pleased about (a classic backhanded breakup move). Well, he figured it out, and even though he'd broken up with me, he was not having any of it. For nearly six months he stood on my lawn, threatening to smash all the windows of my car if I didn't let him in, broke into my voice mail and changed my password so he could listen to my messages, and literally would call me from my driveway demanding to know who was in my house if he had overheard a male voice from outside my window (which was the television, but there was no convincing him of that even after he stormed through every room in my tiny house and searched the backyard). It was freaky, scary, and sad, because this was someone I had really loved, liked, thought was smart, funny, amazing, and all the other things you think about your best friend/boyfriend. Now here he was coming unglued, and nothing his friends or I could do was going to change that. Even when he was dating another girl, he was still showing up at my house at 2 A.M. every night, because "If I can't sleep, then neither can you"—which is a wonderful thing to say. Really a Hallmark moment. Throughout this period of crazy, I didn't tell many people what was happening. I don't know if I felt protective of him or embarrassed that I had so clearly misjudged this person and didn't want to admit it. But after way too many months, I finally realized that being held hostage in my own home every night was ruining my life and there was still no end in sight. I had to lay down the law, as in "If you ever show up here again, I will call the police." After that, he went away.

That was many years ago, and it used to be that when we ran into each other he would glare at me coldly and he and his friends would make a dramatic exit. In the past few years, when I've run into him we've actually talked, and I remember the him that was so funny and appealing. But his expression always betrays the embarrassment he feels about what happened. At least now his friends can tease him about it, and he has enough distance to see how truly cuckoo bananas he was. And weirdly enough, Greg and I ended up having dinner with him in a large group one night unexpectedly, and even Greg really liked him. So now instead of being my "Crazy Ex-Boyfriend," he's become my ex who "seems like a really good guy who just came unglued for a while." But I bet anything he'd love to just be "a great guy I used to date."

APPENDIX

(Or, One More Thing Before We Go)

So you've made it all the way to the end of the book and you're probably thinking, "What else could they possibly have to say?" Only this: that while right now you're nursing a broken heart, you may someday be on the other side of the fence. That's right, you will break up with someone. And when you do, we hope you apply the same thoughtfulness and grace to dumping the poor guy that you've learned to use during your recovery throughout these pages. Let's all do our part to make the world of relationships a little better, and the experience of heartbreak a little easier. With that in mind, here is our own breakup etiquette section so you can be a true Superfox—to yourself and to all mankind:

1. **Don't drag it out.** It's best to do it when you realize that it needs to be done rather than three months or years down the line. Don't waste his time while you figure out your life. Don't

be selfish. Oh, and don't wait for him to break up with you—that's just cruel.

2. **Be definitive.** This is about your feelings, so own them. This is not something that is open for debate, so don't let yourself get talked out of it. You don't want to have to break up with him more than once. One woman said, "Why did he let me talk him out of it? I wish he'd been more firm." Think about how weird it would be to "kind of" get fired from a job. So be direct. Something to the effect of "I wish I felt differently, but this relationship is not something I want to go any further with" or "I'm not feeling like this is the relationship for me." Or some version of the way you talk. You get the point. Deliver the news and make it about your feelings, not a deficit in the other person.

3. **Don't say things that you know will lead him on or give him hope for some future if there is not going to be a future.** This is a common thing that people do to make themselves feel better about having to break up with someone. A great example is "but I hope we can still be friends." Of course you do, we all want to be friends, but if you really want to be a friend to the person you are breaking up with, be clear so they can get on with the healing. Breaking up with someone stinks; getting broken up with stinks more. So if you want to be a friend, think about them.

4. **Be honest yet gracious.** A breakup conversation is not to be used as an opportunity to make a laundry list of everything that was wrong with him and the relationship. Allow him his dignity.

5. **Once you've done the deed, stay away.** Don't check in on

him to ease your own conscience; it just confuses him. Yes, you feel bad; yes, you miss him. But you wanted out, so you don't get to swing by to ease your own temporary pain. Give him the space he needs to hate your guts and get over you so someday maybe you can be friends.

ACKNOWLEDGMENTS

Breakups suck and reliving them is either wildly unpleasant or weirdly humorous. Therefore we'd like to thank all the people who underwent this task for the sake of this book and shared the stories of their breakups with us. We were truly blown away by the generosity of all the people who participated in our breakup surveys. Your stories really helped shape this book. Which is probably what you were hoping for as you went through them, right? None of this would be possible without the hard work and devotion of Julie James, Jon Thoday, Isaac Horne, Carmen Stockton, Andrea Barzvi, Greg Cavic, and Tom Rowan. You guys RAWK! A giant thank-you to Ann Campbell, the smartest, most intuitive, and foxiest editor we could have asked for—your insight and enthusiasm were an invaluable asset to the writing of this book. Thank you to Julia Coblentz, Rex Bonomelli, David Drake, Ursula Cary, and all the folks at Broadway Books—we're happy to have a home with you. A Team Behrendt thank-you to Kristen Behrendt, whose hard work on and off the field made us able to write this book. Liz Tuccillo and Michael Patrick King—we couldn't love you more . . . unless you were made of caramel. Dave "Butterpants" Anthony and Dr. Alex Barzvi, whose input just made this a better book. To the men and women who broke our hearts and gave us the insight into writing this tome. Super Special thanks to Oprah Winfrey, who is . . . well, she's Oprah and we thank her for that.

And, most important, to all our friends and families that stood beside us during our own breakups and encouraged us to run toward the light . . . or the more healthy relationship.